Peace Child International

RESCUE
MISSION
PLANET EARTH

A childrens edition of Agenda 21

In association with the United Nations

UNEP

United Nations Children's Fund

Thank you to our Sponsors

United Nations Children's Fund (UNICEF)   United Nations Development Programme (UNDP)
United Nations Environment Programme (UNEP)   UN Educational, Scientific & Cultural Org. (UNESCO)
Foundation for Environmental Awareness, Hilversum, The Netherlands

Thank you to our adult advisers

Project Coordinator: David Woollcombe, Peace Child International
Assistant: Rosey Simonds, Peace Child International
Publisher: Jane Olliver, Kingfisher Books
Consultants: Koy Thompson, Florian Langenscheidt
Designer: David West

Advisory Committee

Deepak Bajracharya & Andrés Guerrero, UNICEF
Susan Becker, UNDP   Viktor Kolybine, UNESCO   Noel Brown, UNEP

Dedication
To You

First Published on Earth Day 1994 by

KINGFISHER BOOKS
Grisewood & Dempsey Ltd, Elsley House, 24–30 Great Titchfield Street
London W1P 7AD
Grisewood & Dempsey Inc., 95 Madison Avenue, New York
New York 10016

2 4 6 8 10 9 7 5 3   (paperback)
2 4 6 8 10 9 7 5 3 1 (hardback)

British Library Cataloging in Publication Data
for this book is available from the British Library
Library of Congress Cataloging in Publication Data
for this book is available from The Library of Congress
Library of Congress Card Number: 94-20889

ISBN 1-85697-175-9 (paperback)
ISBN 1-85697-174-0 (hardback)

Printed by New InterLitho, Milan, Italy
on chlorine-free paper manufactured from trees grown in sustainable forests

Written, designed, typeset and illustrated by the
Children's Task Force on Agenda 21

The views presented here are those of the authors and not those of the sponsoring organizations

RESCUE MISSION
PLANET EARTH

A children's edition of Agenda 21

by children of the WORLD

In association with the United Nations

THE EDITORS

José Luis Bayer, *Chile*

Andreana Benitez, *The Philippines*

Mia Björkqvist, *Finland*

Birce Boga, *Turkiye(Turkey)*

Hemara Breckenridge, *Switzerland*

Viola Caretti, *Italy*

Victoriano Cerda, *Chile*

Mary Edet, *Nigeria*

Uli Gerza, *Germany*

Tanya Keselj, *Italy*

Jeremy Heimans, *Australia*

Sheku Syl Kamara, *Sierra Leone*

Michael Kanyako, *Sierra Leone*

Ekaterina Kotova, *Russia*

Arancha Diaz Llado, *Spain*

Chamsai Menasveta, *Thailand*

Rekha Menon, *India*

Anuragini Nagar, *India*

Debbie O'Connor, *UK*

Agata Pawlat, *Poland*

Ronnie Pirovino, *USA*

Ivan Sekulovic, *Serbia*

Suhail Sheriff, *Zanzibar, Tanzania*

Blanka Tomancáková, *Czech Republic*

Portia Villanueva, *The Philippines*

Dann Warick, *USA*

Charlotte Wikman, *Finland*

Daniela Zunec, *Croatia*

Kingfisher Books

CONTENTS

INTRODUCTION
Boutros Boutros-Ghali, Secretary-General, United Nations

The Road to Rio
Invitation to the Rescue Mission

EDITORS' NOTE

This is an international book. It includes English as it is spoken and written in England, USA, Australia, Poland, Nigeria, India, Finland etc. We like the variety of styles and made no attempt to smooth it out into one blend of English. Billions here means 1,000 million. Difficult words are explained in a glossary at the back (Glossary = dictionary).

In Parts I and II, we give roughly four pages to each theme, the first two for the problems, the second two for the solutions. The complete list of Agenda 21's chapter titles are listed on Page 95.

About 10,000 kids in about 100 countries contributed to this book plus 50 experts who took the time to be interviewed. Sadly, we only use a fraction of what you gave us. If we'd used it all, this book would have been longer than the original Agenda. Where we know your name, we print it alongside your work. THANK YOU to all contributors.

UNITED NATIONS NATIONS UNIES

Children are among the first victims both of underdevelopment and of environmental degradation. In all countries of the world, rich and poor, they are the first to suffer from poverty, malnutrition, disease and pollution.

It is therefore no coincidence that Agenda 21 contains a special chapter devoted to children and youth in sustainable development, which stresses the need for their active involvement in matters related to environment and development.

Perhaps the major achievement of the Earth Summit was to launch a global partnership for sustainable development. Let us not forget that such a partnership should include and benefit the young, in whose hands lies the future of this planet.

I sincerely hope that this book will help children from all countries better to understand and appreciate the fragile world in which we live and to dedicate themselves to do everything possible to protect and enhance this Earth, our only home.

Boutros Boutros-Ghali
Secretary-General
United Nations

THE ROAD TO RIO

The Rio Summit was the product of global environmental worries which began in 1972. That's when 70 governments met in Stockholm for a conference which created the United Nations Environment Programme or UNEP. UNEP's main job was pushing governments to take more care of the environment. It also hooked up with UNESCO to push environmental education. In 1984, it helped to publish the World Conservation Strategy - a forerunner to Agenda 21. It didn't go into the question of development - the need to balance protecting the environment with people's need for food. So the United Nations appointed a World Commission on Environment and Development which produced the famous report called *Our Common Future* which set out the idea of Sustainable Development. This means:

Meeting the needs of the present without compromising the ability of future generations to meet their needs...

Get it? - Feed the world today but leave a planet around for your great grandchildren. In 1989 the UN decided to hold a conference on Environment and Development. Brazil offered to host it in Rio. For two years, governments, NGOs and experts thrashed out a document that 179 states could agree to. Agenda 21 was the result! It's not a fixed law: no one's going to be punished if they don't do what it says. But the fact that all those governments did agree to it make it very important.

Agata Pawlat, 17, Polan

Hi! We invite you to join the Rescue Mission!

> *The greatest challenge of both our time and the next century is to save the planet from destruction. It will require changing the very foundations of modern civilization - the relationship of humans to nature.*
>
> *Mikhail Gorbachev*

> *As chairman of the Space Sub-committee in the Senate, I strongly urged the establishment of a Mission to Planet Earth, a worldwide monitoring system staffed by children... designed to rescue the global environment.*
>
> *Albert Gore Jnr.*

Gorbachev gives it to us straight: our job in the 21st century is to "save the planet from destruction..." No - this isn't another doom and gloom book about eco-disasters with some kindly advice at the end about how to sort your garbage. This is a book about Agenda 21 - the agenda for the 21st Century agreed by our governments at the Earth Summit in Rio de Janeiro. Never before has something like this happened: a common commitment by 179 different nations.

The original Agenda rambles on for 500 pages and 40 chapters about a $600 billion programme to save the planet. What we've done is to put it into a language that ordinary people can understand. OK, so you're thinking this is another yawn-provoking document from bureaucrats with nothing better to do. Well right, but in it, governments ask for "partnership" with us. With kids! Not for the first time, either: they asked for it at the World Summit for Children *and* in the new law on children's rights which 131 countries have agreed. We decided to take them at their word. Sure let's be partners but equal partners!

We're 28 very different young people from 21 countries but we have one thing in common. We're tired - tired of seeing our beautiful planet polluted, tired of senseless wars, of the poor getting poorer day by day, of waiting for politicians to make decisions they should have made long, long ago.

The Rescue Mission is our wake up call. Al Gore sees it as a way of collecting information about the environment. Fine, but we want to be able to act on that information. Agenda 21 tells you what our governments have agreed: It's a wish list, a dream: we can help make it reality.

So answer YES to our invitation! Join the Rescue Mission by writing to the address on the last page and we'll send you up-to-date news on what's happening in your area.

The Editors, August 1993

Boryana Marinova, 16, Czech Republic

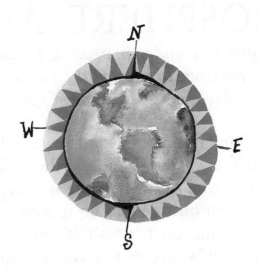

PART I

NATURAL WORLD

ATMOSPHERE ALERT

Our atmosphere is under increasing pressure from greenhouse gases which threaten to change the climate and holes in the ozone layer which cause cancers in humans and animals.

Agenda 21, chapter 9

When the atmosphere is healthy, it is an incredibly wise, self-sufficient system able to adapt to changes. Without this ability, life on Earth would be impossible. It's like the immune system in our bodies: it fights off attacks from outside and up to now, it's been doing pretty well. But its carrying capacity is not unlimited. Human beings have pushed it to a point where its not able to repair its wounds. It is massively traumatized by the greenhouse gases; it is pierced by chloro-fluorocarbons from our fridges and fire extinguishers; it is acidified by sulphur and nitrogen oxides from our cars and factories. The life expectancy of a creature with a damaged immune system is not too hopeful.

A HOLE IN OUR HEARTS

The ozone layer is an essential protective filter in the upper atmosphere that surrounds the Earth. As long as human life has existed, it has protected us from the harmful ultraviolet rays coming from the Sun. When these rays get through the atmosphere, they damage crops, destroy living cells and cause skin cancer. During the last 20 years, ozone levels above Antarctica have decreased by nearly 40% each spring-time. It's all caused mainly by our use of chloro-fluorocar-bons(CFC). Most countries have stopped industry using these in aerosols, but they are still used in other products. The consequences are catastrophic: about 100,000 people die each year from skin cancer. It's especially bad in the Southern hemi-sphere. There is truly no more time to wait: **ALL CFC-use must be stopped immediately!**

Polish Ozone Group

SMOG

Death

Crushed by burden of lead
I breathe in the black particles of
          invisible death
They are surrounding me
          surrounding me from all sides
I keep them away
          with a movement of my hand
I don't see them but
They are still in a terrible nearness
Hidden in mysterious words:
Dioxins, Phenol, Nitrogen Oxides,
Death is lurking,
Encircling every particle of the air
          it kills and kills cruelly
With a black chain which surrounds
My head, my hands, my mind
Death coming with Acid Rain
Turning our world into something
          monstrous
Mutated trees, Dead animals
Black dust swirling over my head
I'm looking for the greenness
          and for the normal trees -
people unchanged into crazies
But only the black smoke
          do I have in sight
Clouds heavy with the poison
There is invisible death
Lurking in them
Invisible Death
Invisible Death
DEATH.....

Aleksandra Warzecka, 17, Poland

Petra Drbalova & Darina Kripalova, Czech Republic

ATMOSPHERE CLEANUP

Governments must get greater energy efficiency out of existing power stations and develop new, renewable energy sources such as solar, wind, hydro, ocean and human power....

Agenda 21, chapter 9

Of the three major atmospheric problems, ozone depletion is the closest to being solved. Not many spray cans use ozone-destroying gases any more but fridges, air conditioners and fire extinguishers do, especially in developing countries: one billion people in the north using ozone-friendly products won't help if four billion people in the South don't. We must get them the new technologies.

The second problem, acid rain, is still killing lakes and forests, often outside the countries which produce the gas. More cooper-ation is needed. On global warming we still have a long way to go. We're not exactly sure what is happening. Finding altern-ative fuels and using energy more efficiently is part of the solution and a major step was taken at Rio with the **Law on Climate Change.** This forces gov-ernments to keep their countries' greenhouse gas production at 1990 levels.

Magdalena Kura,
Polish Ozone Group

Imagine
- with apologies to John Lennon
Imagine there's no nature
Only the stumps of trees.
Only the respirators
To let the creatures breathe,
Imagine all the people
Choking on the air -

You may say that I'm a grumpy
But I'm not the only one
I hope some day you'll join me
And we'll change the Atmosphere!
Polish Ozone Group

I am not an expert. I am just the father of four children who doesn't want my children - or any children - to inherit a world where the air is not fit enough to breathe and where they have to run for cover every time the sun comes out. The politicians of this planet must act soon for if they do not, they will not have a planet left to practise politics on.
Paul McCartney

SPIT-ROASTED PLANET

Ever walked into a greenhouse? It's steamy, humid and it doesn't let up. That's how our world could be in a few decades in the grip of the "greenhouse effect." Gases produced when fossil fuels are burned keep the Sun's heat in and don't let it escape back into space.

That's good up to a point; it gets to be a problem if we keep too much in. We fry! The main "greenhouse gas" is carbon dioxide and we are releasing more and more of it into the atmosphere - 500 billion tons last year! Oceans and forests soak up carbon, so we should hang on to them and stop producing it.

> *There's only one atmosphere. It has no borders. We don't want poisonous gases floating around. We must react. All together.*
> **Child from India**

AGENDA 21 SAYS:
• Promote energy efficiency standards.
• Tax industries in ways that encourage the use of clean, safe technologies.
• Improve substitutes for CFCs and other ozone-depleting substances.
• **Get all these technologies transferred to poor countries!**
• Deal with acid rain that floats across frontiers by having regular exchanges of information, training experts and applying international standards of pollution control.

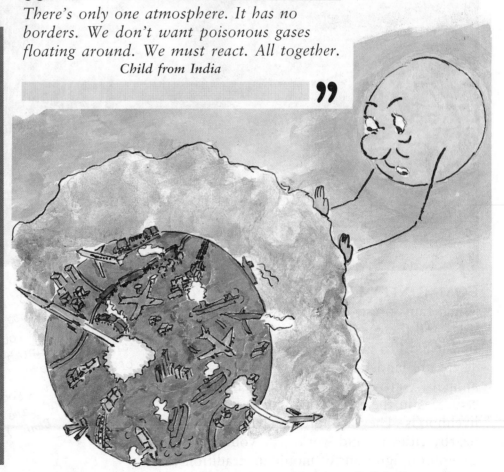

Polish Ozone Group

VANISHING MOUNTAINS

Mountain ecosystems are suffering from soil erosion, landslides and the rapid loss of animals and plant life.

Agenda 21, chapter 13

Mountains are more than just huge rocks decorated with snow. They are homes to whole communities of plants and animals which depend on them for life. When mountain forests are chopped down, these communities crumble away with the earth beneath them. Earth exposed in the wake of deforestation is washed away by rains.

Mountains are vital for more than half the people of the planet who live in the shadow of water or climate systems that flow down from them. If the people and life systems which grow on mountains are vanishing we are under threat.

COMMUNITY EROSION

When rain forests are cut down on mountain sides and the earth is washed away, new trees find it hard to grow in the remaining soil. There are landslides and loss of homes for animals. Native people who have lived for centuries in the mountains also lose their livelihoods. They are forced to move to nearby cities to find work. The younger generation, ignorant of mountain traditions, do not learn from their grandparents how to look after their fragile ecosystems.

Malawi

In my country, people in the mountains are so desperate to find land to cultivate, they tie ropes round their waists and hang off mountain sides to dig the ground and plant seeds. Of course, after a couple of harvests, the good ground falls away leaving behind bare rock.

Benji, 14, Malawi

EXPANDING DESERTS

The results of drought and desertification include poverty and starvation. About three million people died in the mid-1980s because of drought in Africa south of the Sahara.

Agenda 21, chapter 12

Desertification! The word conjures up an image of sand dunes rolling across farms and villages, turning everything into a desert. Wrong! Deserts expand and contract with the weather. People who have farmed the deserts for centuries know this. The real problem that needs to be addressed is "soil degradation" - the way good land slowly becomes less and less fertile. This is an increasing problem affecting a quarter of the land area of the planet and a billion people! It's caused by climate change, drought and political changes that stop poor people from owning their land and nomads from grazing their herds over lands they have "farmed" for centuries.

Polish Ozone Group

Bad management of livestock is eating our future!

Agata Pawlat, 17, Poland

A carnage of death

The soil around my village is changing colour. The army moves in and tells us that land my ancestors have farmed for centuries is no longer our's. Miners come and destroy much land to extract precious minerals. Poachers pursue wildlife to the point of extinction. All leave behind a carnage of death in my country. They care nothing for international regulations. No police can stop them: the police are in the pay of the poachers and miners!

Ernest, 19, Ghana

BRING BACK THE EARTH!

Poverty is a major factor in soil degradation. We need to restore fragile lands and find new jobs for farmers thrown out of work...

Agenda 21, chapter12

Yes, but how? - unfortunately Agenda 21 is not rich in solutions. "There's insufficient knowledge of desertfication processes..." seems to be the conclusion. "Strengthen the knowledge base..." Find out what on earth is going on!

The other thing to do is to get everyone from governments to local farmers and their families to know what's going on and involved in deciding and doing what needs to be done.

Target: June 1994
International Convention on Desertification.

Much negotiation is happening at the UN to see this happen. It will be a law which forces the International Community to do the things that the Agenda proposes and provide money to do it. *(At the moment, there is very little money available from international banks for desertification.)*

African countries, where desertification is a serious problem, very much want a new convention, but rich countries, who would have to pay for it, don't. They offered a deal: "We'll sign the desert convention if you sign one on forests."

No deal yet, but there needs to be one: failure would mean more millions of hectares of good land becoming degraded and many millions of people being condemned to lives of poverty.

AGENDA 21 SAYS:

• Increase knowledge of mountain and desert ecosystems by having a world information centre and identify areas most at risk from floods, soil erosion etc.
• Give farmers environmental education.
• Prevent desertification by not polluting soil, by using land soundly and by planting of trees that retain water and soil quality.
• Pass laws to protect endangered areas.
• Make plans to ensure that potential drought victims survive.

Target: Year 2000

Mountain Strategy

This will be like a local Agenda 21 for all mountain areas. It will have farm plans, plans for employment, eco-tours, environmentally sound mining plans + social infrastructure and transport systems.

The Cranes
Anna Rumyantseva, 13, Russia

&&

Take time to pause and reflect. In daily life, we are bombarded with information from many sources. News directs our attention to problems. We have lost our natural instincts, our intuitions.

We have to rediscover our relationship with nature: go back to the majesty of the mountains.

Rediscover the magnificent emptiness of the deserts. Here in the Alps, the pendulum is swinging back towards quality tourism where people respect nature.

Sadruddin Aga Khan, Switzerland

&&

CHAINSAW MASSACRE

Forests worldwide are now threatened by uncontrolled exploitation by human beings. They are being turned into farms or destroyed for timber and other uses.

Agenda 21, chapter 11

A forest is more than a neat arrangement of matchsticks. In the Amazon rain forest, a scientist found that a single tree provides a home for two thousand unique species of animals. Forests are vital to our global ecosystems: they act as sinks for carbon dioxide. Rip them away and humans could not survive. In many countries, especially developing ones, forests are vital to the larger social and economic picture: millions of trees are cut down every year in the name of survival. Logging, agriculture, fire, acid rain - all conspire to destroy forests. But in the tropical rain forests - it's a massacre.

Ragamuffin Nature, Tink again
All de people man dem, tink again
before burning down de forest, tink again
to build de house man, tink again
before to cut de trees man, tink again

Tink all da people or some o dem
once de forest will go
de desert will come again
As de increase in a de CO2 will make de
world hotter so making life some shorter

Man me say tink again, tink about de
desert de oxygen and de flower
All de people me say loudly, tink again
    Amish K. Shah, Tanzania

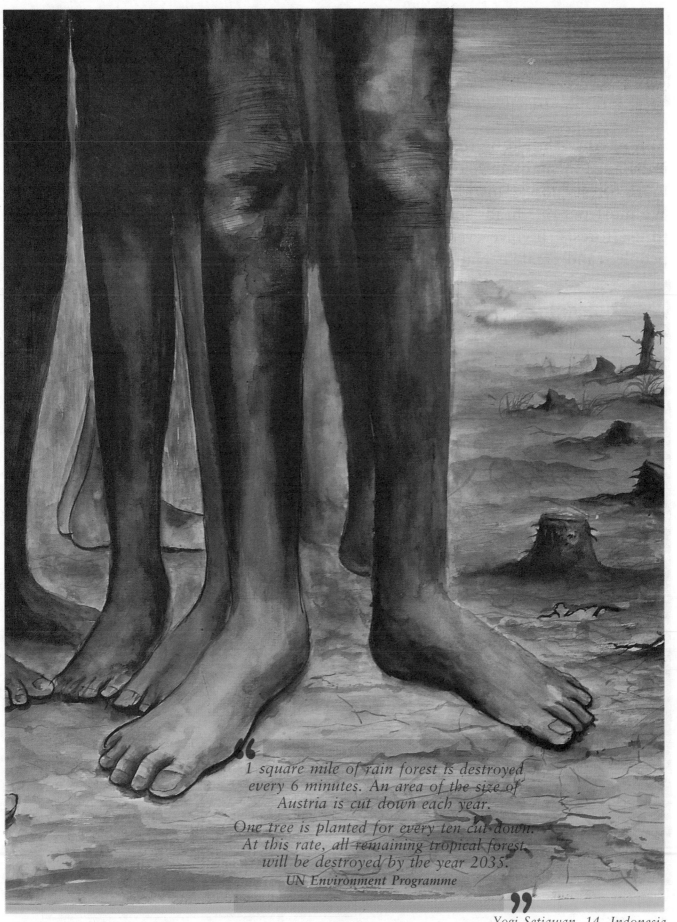

"1 square mile of rain forest is destroyed every 6 minutes. An area of the size of Austria is cut down each year.

One tree is planted for every ten cut down. At this rate, all remaining tropical forest will be destroyed by the year 2035.
UN Environment Programme"

Yogi Setiawan, 14, Indonesia

THE SEEDS OF CHANGE

Forests need to be preserved for their social and spiritual values, including the traditional habitats of indigenous people, forest dwellers and local communities. Agenda 21, chapter 11

Top priority should be to do something about the environmental imbalance in many developing countries. Conserve and plant more forests now! This idea is equally important for rich nations. We must put our heads together and find new, sustainable ways to use forests. Involve everyone - women, youth, indigenous people - and create a National Forest Action Plan for every country.

Forests from scratch

A little known village in India named Karnaka has set an example by building a small but thick wood forest. The people of the village pledged not to cut one tree. They protect the forest every moment and without any assistance from the Forest Department; in fact, they do not even allow the forest officials inside.

Anuragini Nagar, 19, India

Anon, UK

REDUCE, RECYCLE, RE-USE!

In our community, we use and re-use things until they are completely worn out. For example, glass bottles are used again and again for water storage. Polythene bags are washed and used many times. Re-use is an idea the West can borrow from the developing world. It sure is the cheapest form of recycling.

Suhail Sheriff, Zanzibar, Tanzania

Planting trees is sometimes better than recycling

Recycling, that great environmental saviour, may not be as beneficial as it seems. In Thailand, all paper is recycled. The old paper has to be washed to get rid of all the ink and this causes heavy metals to pollute Thailand's rivers. The poison gets into the fish and the surrounding countryside. The best thing is always to plant fresh trees.

Rauno Laithalainen, Thai Forestry Worker

Tamara Rossi, 13, Italy

AGENDA 21 SAYS:

• **Plant new forests!!**
• Practical knowledge on the state of forests is needed: planners often lack even basic information on size and types of trees in forests.
• Further research is needed into forest products like wood, fruits, nuts, dyes, medicines, gums etc.
• Replant damaged areas of woodland;
• Breed trees that are more resistant to environmental pressures.
• Local business people should be encouraged to set up small forest enterprises.
• Limit and aim to stop slash-and-burn farming methods.
• Keep wood waste to a minimum. Find ways of using trees that have been burnt or thrown out.
• Increase tree-planting in urban areas.

SEA OF TROUBLES

Oceans are under increasing stress from pollution, over-fishing and general degradation. It affects everything from the climate to coral reefs.

Agenda 21, chapter 17

Our seas are under intense pressure from pollution, most of which comes from human beings. Like the atmosphere, it is incredibly flexible, but we are pushing it to its limits. It's going to get worse: by the year 2020, three-quarters of us will be living 60km (40 miles) from a coastline. If we don't change, those extra people will be pouring sewage and waste into the seas.

600,000 tons of oil is junked into the sea by ships every year as a matter of course! No wonder many of the fish we are catching are unfit to eat. That doesn't stop us trying to catch them. Some use huge, mile-long drift nets that catch dolphins and other things we don't need. Over-fishing means worldwide fish catches are dropping.

Harri Sara & Antte Aarnio, Finland

Hong Kong

CASE STUDY 21

Bathing in the sea now is not a pleasure at all in Hong Kong. Untreated sewage is constantly found in seas. Visitors have to reluctantly keep away and swim in pools instead.

The water quality in Rambler Channel is getting worse at an alarming rate. There's zero oxygen in the water and a lot of mud contaminated mud poisonous metals....

Red tides off the East Coast of Hong Kong are killing hundreds of fish. Red tides are big plumes of algae, the stuff that turns ponds and rivers green. In the sea, it's a rust red colour, not poisonous, but it sucks oxygen out of the water and kill tons of fish and seals. In Hong Kong, they are killing all the fish in the fish farms. Bad for business.

Livingstone School, Hong Kong

Ekaterina Kotova, 15, Russia

The Mermaids

I saw the mermaids
Crawl up on the shore
They couldn't live longer
Down there any more

They had horrible stories
Of what's going on there
The scenes that they witnessed
Which they couldn't bear

They told of a black cloud
That sometimes spread on top
From which strange black rain
Towards them did drop

They also saw huge nets
Rumbling in the deep
Dragging all inside them
Big and small fish to keep.

Dorothy Sciberras, Malta

Miho Uchida, Japan

LIFE IN THE OCEAN WAVES

Nations must commit themselves to control and reduce the pollution of the marine environment and maintain its life support capacity.
Agenda 21, chapter 17

People have to stop thinking of our seas as an unlimited treasure chest of treasure waiting for us to plunder. We have to stop vacuum-cleaning the seas dry of fish. We understand far less about the delicate ecosystems of the ocean than we do about those on dry land. We have to study it more - and respect it like we respect the rain forest. It is the home of millions of animals who have as much right to life as us.

AGENDA 21 SAYS:
• Protect and check environmental damage to coastal areas nationally and internationally.
• Polluters should pay for the damage they cause. Those using cleaner methods should be rewarded.
• Protect marine life by controlling what materials may be removed from ships at sea and by banning removal of hazardous waste.
• Nations should share new technologies.
• Set limit on how many fish may be caught.
• Encourage fishing by skilled local people.
• Stop fishing for species at risk until they are back up to their normal numbers.
• Ban destructive fishing practices - dynamiting, poisoning and others; develop new practices to replace them.

Ekaterina Kotova, 15, Russia

Take care!
The earth is dead without water
Man is dead without water
Birds, fishes, sheep, goats, cows and all
They are dead without water
The sea and the river
They give us love and joy
The ocean keeps the world together
Where are we without these?
I will reach out in my boat to yonder land
Because the sea gives me road
The oceans and rivers give me road
So take care of our marine areas
Please! - take care!
Dudley Fewry, 18, Sierra Leone

Elif Uysal, Malta

SMALL ISLAND STATES

Small island states are in the worst condition of all. Stuck in the middle of the oceans, cut off from the rest of the world, they depend mostly on the sea for their livelihood. If the sea level rises due to global warming, some of these states may disappear completely.

AGENDA 21 SAYS:
• Prepare sustainable development plans for small island states.
• Support the islands' indigenous culture.
• Set up high-level policy-making bodies to cooperate with Non-Governmental groups to put these plans into effect.

RIVERS OF SHAME

All social and economic activity relies heavily on fresh water. Water is becoming scarce in many countries. The management of water resources is of paramount importance in the 1990s and beyond...

Agenda 21, chapter 18

It's no accident that the two longest chapters in Agenda 21 deal with rivers and seas. The "Earth Summit" might better have been called a "Water Summit" as our planet is 70% water and it is water, or the lack of it, which will cause many problems in the 21st Century. In dry areas like the Middle East, nations threaten to go to war about it.

WATER SHORTAGES

Today many countries have less water than they need. Early in the next century, a third of the world's nations will be permanently short of water.

Where are new sources of water? As forests are cut down, springs dry up. Underground lakes, laid down in prehistoric times, are running down fast.

We are taking about as much water as we can from rivers. Pollution cripples much of the rest.

Desalinating sea water is a possible source but it costs ten times as much to make.

CASE STUDY 21

Germany

When I go canoeing in Plettenburg, I get horrified by the things I see around me - bikes, fridges, cars - just dumped in the river. A lot of factories take water from these rivers to cool their machines: what they pump back is not only water but also chemicals, oil, rubbish, junk. Sometimes, it's horrible to just be near the river, it smells so bad ...

Gabriel, 14, Germany

Satoko Ishii, 11, Japan

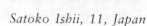

SOME FOR ALL

By the year 2000, all city people should be provided with 40 litres of safe drinking water daily. By the year 2025, there should be safe water and sanitation for all. Agenda 21, chapter 18

A drop
*Nothing more than a drop and in it -
Everything! A whole world
Transparent but full, wet and alive
One sphere meets a universe of water
Glowing in brilliant colours
Unattainable and always present.*

*Listening to the moving waves
I feel the peace inside myself.
But the perfume-flavored, man-made drop
I cannot swallow.
Toilets flush,
House water bubbles.
The inebriated captain crashes the tanker.*
Anon. USA

Shinnosuke Sugiyama, 13, Japan

PROBLEM FAMILY

Biological resources feed and clothe us, provide us with housing, medicines and spiritual nourishment. The loss of biodiversity continues at a faster rate as a result of human activity.

Agenda 21, chapter 15

What is Biodiversity? Bio means life, as in Biology, the science of life. Diversity means variety so biodiversity means the variety of life - 30 million species according to one estimate. Trouble is, one species seems intent on wiping out the other 29,999,999. People need what plants and animals provide: for example, a drug that comes from the rose-colored periwinkle of Madagascar, has helped many people recover from leukaemia (a kind of cancer). By our lack of respect for other life forms around us, we are gradually killing the ecosystems that give us life.

Senya Perebaeva, 12, Russia

Mother Nature
I am mother nature,
the lasting habitat of destruction
I am a creation of heaven, from heaven I am
given for man to dwell and to toil.
But man, in complete disregard of truth, has
chosen to destroy all my children.
Greed and hate, the nagging times of age,
have flamed the heart of man.
The ravages of war and factory are
the friendly foe of man.
The young earth's fervant destroyer is
the fumes of the factory.
The water animals happily sing the songs of life,
while we send our nets to fish their families
in entirety.
But know you not man that in your greed you
may destroy all my off springs?
Yet in destroying me, you pave a smooth way to
your own destruction.
Repent now from your greed and protect the
sons and daughters of mother nature.
The value of a shade will not be known until
the tree is cut down.

Sheku Kamara, 20, Sierra Leone

THE GOOD STEWARD

I dream of a world in which people want to save the rose-colored periwinkle of Madagascar for its own sake, not because it happens to contain a cure for cancer in people.

Children's State of the Planet Handbook 1992

BIODIVERSITY CONVENTION

A lot of these ideas are included in the Biodiversity Convention which will soon become a law. 142 countries signed the Convention at Rio but it doesn't become a law until at least 30 countries *ratify* it - that is make it a law in their own countries. By August 1993, 26 countries had ratified it. The USA signed it in April 1993.

AGENDA 21 SAYS:
- *one thing: SAVE IT!! In order to do that, governments have to:*
• Create a world information resource for biodiversity.
• Protect biodiversity! This should be a part of all government plans on environment and development.
• Offer indigenous peoples the chance to contribute to biodiversity conservation.
• Make sure that poor countries share equally in the commercial exploitation of their products and experience.
• Protect and repair damaged habitats; conserve endangered species.
• Assess every big project - dams, roads etc. - for its environmental impact.

Jennifer Zee, Hong Kong

Ece Toraman, 7, Turkiye (Turkey)

PART II

HUMAN WORLD

BABY BOMB

The world's growing population and unsustainable consumption patterns are putting increasing stress on air, land, water and energy resources.

Agenda 21, chapter

Did you know that within the time it takes to draw one breath, 500 kids are born. No, the solution is not to stop breathing. We have to stop the trend of rapid population growth. Our planet cannot cope with it much longer: if we do nothing, the world population will level off close to 14-15 billion at the end of the next century - three times what it is today! We're finding it quite a challenge to feed, house and clothe 5 billion, but three times that number....?

Shrikant Mansing Pawar, 11, India

Brain Drain

The most horrible problem in our country at the moment is unemployment. For every 100 people, able and willing to do a job, 15 cannot find one. Population growth makes it impossible to fill the gap between the employed and the unemployed. People are compelled to do jobs for which they are over-qualified, so they join the brain drain to seek jobs abroad. As population grows in other countries, there will be nowhere for them to drain to...

Heluaki, Sri Lanka

" *The planet groans every time it registers another birth.*

Paul Simon, Born at the Right Time "

Q *Agenda 21 chapter 5 on population is very weak. How did this happen?*

A It happened because very powerful lobbies did not allow the Summit to reach agreement about the population issue. At the same time, several major developed countries did not want to talk about the other side of the population issue, which is consumption. The result was that there was no concensus on either.

Shridath Ramphal, co-chair,
Commission on Global Governance

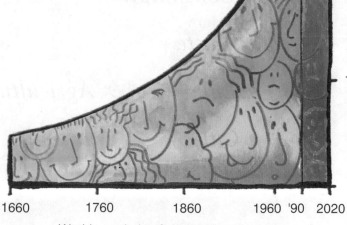

World population from 1660 projected to the year 2020. (In billions)

Wendy Vilma Figueroa Cedón, 14, Peru

INDIVIDUAL CHOICE

Countries need to know their national population carrying capacity - how many people their countries can hold without bursting.　　　Agenda 21, chapter 5

Women are at the centre of the population growth problem. It is they who have babies. But why is it that in the developed world, women have 1-2 children while in the developing world, they have 5 or more? Two reasons:

1. EDUCATION

66

If you take a thousand girls in Africa and give them one more year of primary education, they will have 500 less children. The link between education and family size has been proven time and time again. To educate a girl in Africa at the primary level costs about US$35 per year - which is the best use of $35 anywhere in the world.　　　**Andrew Steer, World Bank.**

99

2. ECONOMICS

If you know your one child will survive, you won't feel the need to have five.

66

In Kenya population doubles every 18 years. People have children for fairly good reasons. Children are an economic advantage from the age of seven onwards-they earn more than they consume. High infant mortality means you have to have lots of children so that at least some will reach adulthood. It used to be said in India that you had to have six children to be sure that one, preferably a son, would survive.

Geoffrey Lean, The Observer

99

POPULATION PROGRAMMES

People in the Third World countries do not have big families because they are careless or ignorant. Children are their hope. Their only security. Because they don't have any control over their fertility, they end up with too many children. What they need is the information and the means to control the size of their families. In other words, population programmes.

Careful! This is more than just distributing contraception. It's about the whole economic and social situation. The smallest families happen in the most secure societies, where there is peace, economic and political security and education systems. Most of all, they happen where women are treated as equal citizens, with equal access to well-paying jobs and education.

Q *There's a lot in Agenda 21 about women playing a critical role in population, but aren't men usually the problem?*

A Yes - there's a lot of male authority but not much male responsibility in relation to child bearing. Men are not burdened with the problem of giving birth, they tend to exploit children - sending them to work instead of investing in their education. What can children do? They should challenge their parents not to have any more children until they can look after them properly.

Dr Nafis Sadik, Executive Director,
UN Population Fund

SPARE A SPACE, PLEASE!

Marco De Leon, 8, Philippines

SICK TO DEATH

Human health depends on a healthy environment, clean water supply, sanitary waste disposal, adequate shelter and a good supply of healthy food.

Agenda 21, chapter 6

Never in history has knowledge of medicine been greater than it is today. Genetics, organ transplant-ations, immunology, improved antibiotics and vitamins, discovery of insulin and cortisone etc, etc.

BUT - still 3 million children die each year from preventable diseases. About half a million women die each year from causes related to pregnancy and child birth. Minimal health care is still beyond the reach of more than a million of the world's poor people.

Hundreds of millions of people have chronic sickness caused by over-crowding in cities and general urban pollution.

"Something"
This is something solid
Something liquid
Something within.
This is something that helps life begin.
Without this something, nothing can endure.
This is something that is naturally pure.
But somehow today this is not true.
What could the problem be?
Could it be you?
Could it be me?

Keelan Kirkland,   USA

A I D S

What? AIDS stands for Acquired Immune Deficiency Syndrome. In simple language, it means your body cannot heal its own sickness. No ways have yet been found to cure it.

How? AIDs is caused by Human Immunodeficiency Virus (HIV) transmitted through the bloodstream by injections, blood transfusions or by having sex with an infected person, male or female. It can also be passed from an infected mother to an unborn child. It cannot be transmitted by kissing, sharing dishes or dirty toilets.

Who? The majority of the HIV infected people are 15 to 49 years of age. The number of infected people is growing constantly. The USA has by far the highest number of reported AIDS cases, nearly half of all the world's total. But in African countries like Malawi, Tanzania and Uganda, the number of cases in proportion to the population is already double that of the USA. The number is increasing in Asia, Latin America and the Caribbean.

So what? The problem is colossal. In the developed world, the trauma of AIDs is tearing apart whole families; the cost of treating each patient is placing heavy strain on health care systems. In the developing world, it's far worse: AIDs affects mainly the educated classes. It threatens to wipe out the very people who can lead their countries and their economies into the 21st Century.

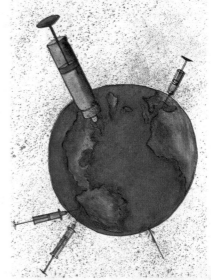

Ekaterina Kotova, 15, Russia

It's about bringing consciousness into our sex lives - when we do it, with whom, in what way, with what protection. It's about making sure people have choices and know enough to make good ones.

*Alan Atkisson,
In Context magazine*

Breathing in Silesia is bad for your health

The air in Upper Silesia is contaminated by thousands of chemicals. The level of health education and social awareness is very low. The children are ill because their parents live in a contaminated environment, breathe contaminated air, drink the contaminated water and often smoke and work in contaminated conditions.

Deformities and mutations are the most visible results of this. Babies and animals are born with three legs, four arms, deformed heads and irregular bone structures. Even if they are born normal, heavy metals and radiation are dangerous for babies in their early days of life.

Children's Parliament of Silesia

FIRST AID

Sound development is not possible without a healthy population but the lack of development makes many health problems far worse. The overall goal is Health for All by the Year 2000.

Agenda 21, chapter 6

Health for all by the year 2000? Sounds unreal, doesn't it? However, the Agenda points a way basing health care in local communities: governments must help them develop their own community-based primary health care. Also, respect for traditional ways of healing is essential.

" *In Sierra Leone there are government hospitals, private hospitals and herbalists.*

Government ones are short of medicine; private ones are very expensive and the medicines they sell are western made. In this situation, Africans rely on herbalists - the use of roots, leaves and barks from trees which is faster and more effective than modern medicines.
Michael, 19, Sierra Leone

"

Ma Myat San Moe, 14, Myanmar

AGENDA 21 SAYS:

Health for all by 2000 requires that we:

• Eliminate guinea-worm disease, polio, river blindness and leprosy completely.
• Reduce and control tuberculosis and measles, and cut childhood deaths due to diarrhoea by 50-70%.
• Protect mothers. Provide them with the means to choose the number and spacing of their babies; allow them to breast-feed their babies for the first 4 months of life.
• Immunize all children; protect them from sexual and workplace exploitation.
• Use effective traditional knowledge in national health care systems.

• All nations to identify environmental health hazards and take steps to reduce them.
• Coordinate national efforts to control the spread of the HIV "Aids" virus.
• Put anti-malaria programmes in place everywhere malaria is still a problem.
• Establish standards for industrial hygiene, use of pesticides, maximum permitted safe noise and exposure levels to ultraviolet radiation.
• Protect vulnerable groups, particularly the elderly and disabled population.

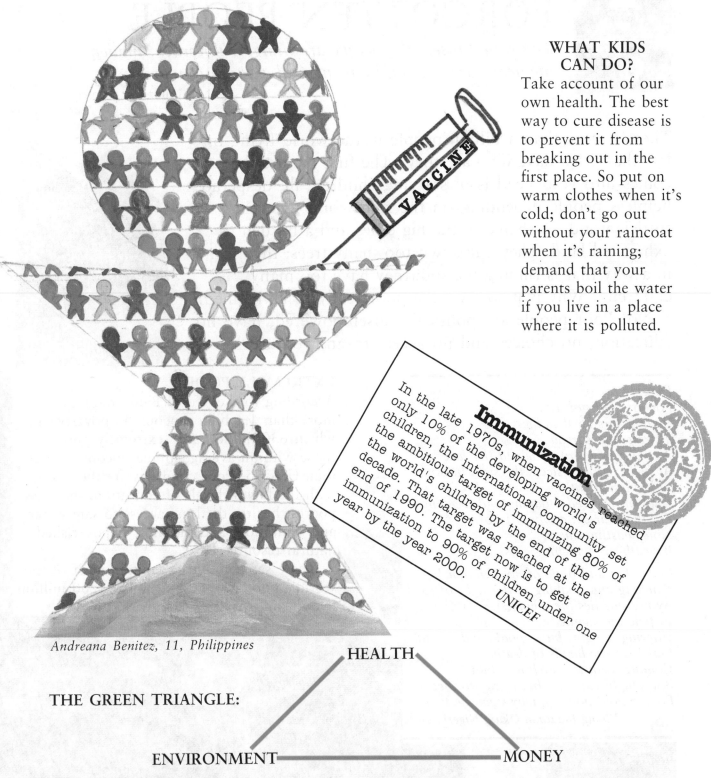

Andreana Benitez, 11, Philippines

WHAT KIDS CAN DO?

Take account of our own health. The best way to cure disease is to prevent it from breaking out in the first place. So put on warm clothes when it's cold; don't go out without your raincoat when it's raining; demand that your parents boil the water if you live in a place where it is polluted.

Immunization

In the late 1970s, when vaccines reached only 10% of the developing world's children, the international community set the ambitious target of immunizing 80% of the world's children by the end of the decade. That target was reached at the end of 1990. The target now is to get immunization to 90% of children under one year by the year 2000.

UNICEF

THE GREEN TRIANGLE:

HEALTH

ENVIRONMENT —————————— MONEY

How do you like this? It's called *The Green Triangle*. Almost any action you take in your life produces an effect on the three corners of the triangle. Example: you choose to eat rich meaty food. It's bad for your health; it damages the environment, and it costs you more money.

Another example: you start walking or bicycling instead of using your car. Results: pollution emissions are cut down - good for the environment; your health improves and you save money on gas.

Fun, isn't it? So whatever you do, check it out first on the green triangle!

FORGOTTEN PEOPLE

The root causes of poverty are hunger, illiteracy, inadequate medical care, unemployment and population pressures.

Agenda 21, chapter 3

There's more than a billion people in the world living on less than $1 a day. Who are they? The first picture that comes into your head is of starving children, ill, desperate, helpless people depending on the rich world's never sufficient aid - a shame to the big cities and a burden to exhausted land. They cut down too many trees; they farm in a way that is ruining the soil; they have too many children... Why is it so? Are the poor really to be blamed?

No! Poor people are politically disempowered, have no education, no choices and no access to any resources.

Poverty

Poverty, oh! poverty!
Your letters spell sadness,
distress and sorrow.
Awaking at morn, I behold thy face.
At night before I sleep, thy sight bids me
a sleepless night.
I lay on my bed moaning and weeping.
For the dear child whom I bore,
Now wasting away,
Beneath my watching eyes.

Only skin and bone of my children I see
Yawning and quaking at the sight of food.
By my side lies the youngest
so pale and white
Uttering naught, but "food! food!"
Oh! I see the hands of death,
Coming forth to clutch my child
But naught can I do but to say to thee
Poverty, oh! poverty, why treat me thus?

Ubong Jonathan Okan, Nigeria

EXTREMELY POOR

According to the World Bank, there are more than 1.1 billion people in poverty of which 630 million are "extremely poor" - those with an average annual income of less than US$275. Poor countries are the ones with the lowest levels of education, the poorest health, the least access to safe water and sanitation, and the most impoverished natural resource base.

These same countries contain most of the world's poor people, but not all. 200 million live in industrialized countries.

Step over him

Step over him like he's not even there
Nevermind his sunken stare
He's here 'cause he wants to be here
Any money you give him he'll waste on beer
He ain't our problem-he's no one we know
Our taxes build shelters, that's where he'll go.
Another bum on the street makes no difference to me
I work for a living. So can he.
He's not really a man, just trash in the way
They should sweep'em all up and throw 'em away
Just another piece of litter, that's all I see.
...Oh, please God, don't let that happen to me.
        D. J. Purnell, 14, USA

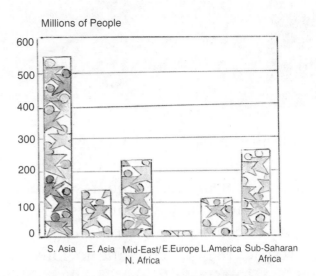

Millions of People

This is where the poorest people of the world live.

RICH vs. POOR
You might have thought that over the last 30 years, the gap between the richest and the poorest on our planet would have narrowed. Wrong! It's twice as big now as it was in 1960. Our world has 157 billionaires, 2 million millionaires and 1.1 billion who live on less than $1 a day.

POVERTY ROCKS!

The main aim of anti-poverty programmes is to make poor people better able to earn a living in a sustainable way.

Agenda 21, chapter 3

People in the developed world think of the poor as people to be pitied, people to give money to. Wrong! Agenda 21's key message is that the poor are incredibly resourceful - they have to be, to be able to live in horrible environments on $200 a year. Most rich, so-called educated people would die! We must give the poor the respect they deserve and include them as full and equal partners in the search for solutions.

CASE STUDY 21

Third World Shops

Have you ever thought about from where your morning coffee comes from? Or who's picked the banana you're having as a snack? Do you have any idea how much the guy who picked makes per bunch? An average banana picker in Brazil earns about US $.50¢ an hour.

So where does the money in between disappear? To multinational companies. Typical products sold by multinationals include coffee, tea, chocolate, tropical fruits and spices.

The Third World Shop movement is trying to break this post-colonial chain of oppression by offering developing countries fair trading conditions. The shops buy ready-processed products directly from small, third world co-operatives. By avoiding middle-men, they can pay reasonable prices. Staff in Third World Shops are usually voluntary. We like to help developing countries in an active way, giving maximum advantage to the poor countries we have exploited so long.

Mia, 19, Finland

> It's wrong to think that only the rich can give help. Anybody can. The right gesture comes from the heart, not from the pocket.
>
> *Mr Dinadayalan, Social Welfare and Nutritious Meal Program, Tamil Nadu, India*

FAIR TRADE NOT JUST AID

What the poor lack is resources. They don't usually need to be given these. They are well able to earn them if they are given a fair deal in the trading system. What happens now is that rich governments allow a log to come in with low customs taxes but a chair, something that's been through a factory, has very high taxes. This means it's not worth poor countries building factories to make logs into chairs although they could do it much more cheaply than rich countries.

This is called protectionism. Closing the doors of the world's markets to the poor. We must open the doors. Until we do, all the aid in the world will not end poverty.

SHOP 'TIL YOU ..

The major cause of the continued deterioration of the global environment is the unsustainable pattern of consumption and production, particularly in the industrialized countries.

Agenda 21, chapter 4

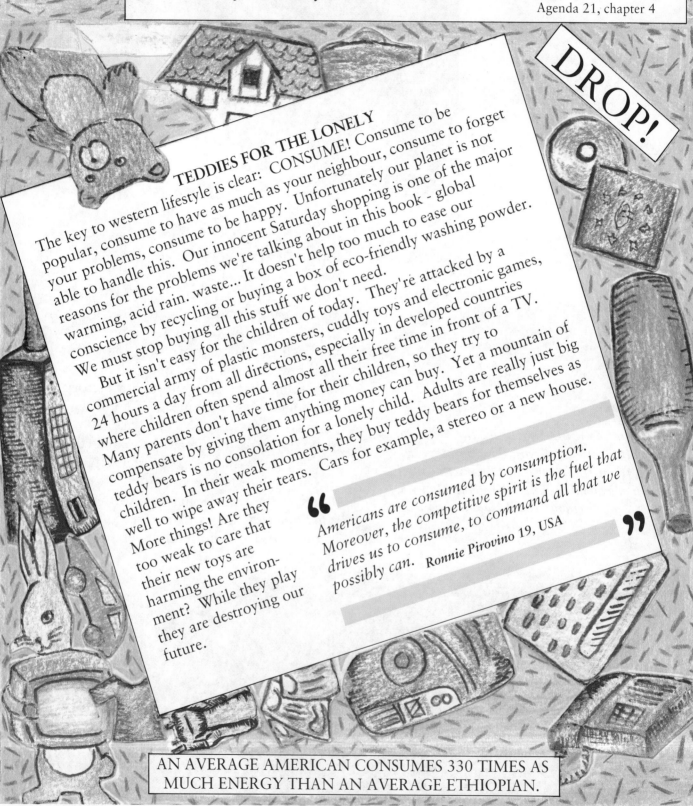

DROP!

TEDDIES FOR THE LONELY

The key to western lifestyle is clear: CONSUME! Consume to be popular, consume to have as much as your neighbour, consume to forget your problems, consume to be happy. Unfortunately our planet is not able to handle this. Our innocent Saturday shopping is one of the major reasons for the problems we're talking about in this book - global warming, acid rain, waste... It doesn't help too much to ease our conscience by recycling or buying a box of eco-friendly washing powder. We must stop buying all this stuff we don't need.

But it isn't easy for the children of today. They're attacked by a commercial army of plastic monsters, cuddly toys and electronic games, 24 hours a day from all directions, especially in developed countries where children often spend almost all their free time in front of a TV. Many parents don't have time for their children, so they try to compensate by giving them anything money can buy. Yet a mountain of teddy bears is no consolation for a lonely child. Adults are really just big children. In their weak moments, they buy teddy bears for themselves as well to wipe away their tears. Cars for example, a stereo or a new house. More things! Are they too weak to care that their new toys are harming the environment? While they play they are destroying our future.

> *Americans are consumed by consumption. Moreover, the competitive spirit is the fuel that drives us to consume, to command all that we possibly can.* Ronnie Pirovino 19, USA

AN AVERAGE AMERICAN CONSUMES 330 TIMES AS MUCH ENERGY THAN AN AVERAGE ETHIOPIAN.

Chamsai Menasveta, 17, Thailand

TURNING UP THE HEAT

We are addicted to energy. We want to buy more, newer, bigger, better things; we want to drive all over in our own cars; we want to fly whenever it's possible. This comfortable life costs energy and the more we use, the bigger the threat to the environment. The use of fossil fuel (coal, oil, gas) results in acid rain and the greenhouse effect: hurricanes, floods and the rising of the sea level. These threats are serious. The sea level is rising at ten times its natural speed. This can result in whole countries disappearing! Still fossil fuels are the most popular energy source. It's hard to use less. Nuclear power has failed to provide a safe alternative. The big question is what happens when developing countries start requiring the luxuries enjoyed in the developed world? If we used as much energy per person as industrialized countries, the world would need five times as much as it uses today. Our planet definitely couldn't stand the pollution this would generate. So what should we in the developing world do? Shut up, stay poor. No way! We must find new *sustainable* sources of energy and so must the industrialized countries.

José Luis Bayer, Chile

CHILL OUT !

We've got to develop new concepts of wealth and prosperity which are more in harmony with the Earth's carrying capacity.

Agenda 21, chapter 4

The main responsibility for cutting down consumption and energy use lies with industrialized countries. They must cut it NOW - instead of constantly increasing it.

AGENDA 21 SAYS:

- Reduce consumption; use less energy.
- Eco-label less harmful products.
- Make eco-friendly products cheaper by taxing eco-harmful ones.
- Tax industry that pollutes or spoils limited nature resources; support eco-friendly industry.
- Develop sources of renewable energy.
- Help developing countries in building their economies based on utilizing renewable sources of energy.

WHAT CAN WE DO?

The best thing to do is, simply: don't buy anything that isn't necessary. And when you must buy, choose a product that is as eco-friendly as possible. When making your decision, think of what has happened before the stuff got to your hands (how it was made, of what material, using how much energy, in what kind of working conditions), as well as what will happen when you won't need it any more (can you compost or recycle it, or maybe pass it to a friend).

The business world produces only what people want to buy. The decisions you make when doing your everyday shopping can have a bigger effect than you could imagine!

Solar Box Cookers

Invented in California, these portable cookers can be used to cook family meals anywhere there is continuous sunshine. Advantages are obvious:

- no need to cut down trees;
- no polluting fires;
- no hot surfaces to burn children;
- simple to make;
- real cheap to run!

Every home should have one!

Peace Child Santa Cruz, USA

José Luis Bayer, Chile

THE BEST THINGS IN LIFE ARE FREE

What we need is to find a new kind of lifestyle based on inner instead of outer values. To find a reason for living other than collecting as much material things as possible.

This can also be a chance for us to discover something new about ourselves. When we look back, we might notice that the best moments in our lives were not bought ones.

> *We should act more as human beings and not like human havings. Human havings are dependent of the power status that people would recognize in you if you have more cars, a bigger home or whatever. But, if you can accept that you're a human being, then you just are.*
>
> Fred Matser, Harmony Health Centre, Netherlands

*Joanna
Michalik,
Poland*

MY HAPPIEST MOMENTS ...

- *are in the open fields, seeing the wonders of nature. In nature, I find joy, love and freedom. Oh! trees, I get a particular joy when I see you moving your leaves, the rivers moving slowly and the long sandy beaches with their ebbing tide.*

It all started when I was a small boy. My parents talked to me about the need to protect the environment. From that moment, I had the longing to be amongst other youth around the world working towards a solution to our environment problems. Working on this book has been certainly the happiest time in my life. Just sitting together around a table, mapping out plans to free the trees, the rivers, the beaches from destruction, and to hear people in the North so concerned about the future of Youth in the South. That, for me, is better than all the fast cars, big houses or so called "jet-set" life style.

Sheku Syl Kamara, 20, Sierra Leone

DANGEROUS GARBAGE

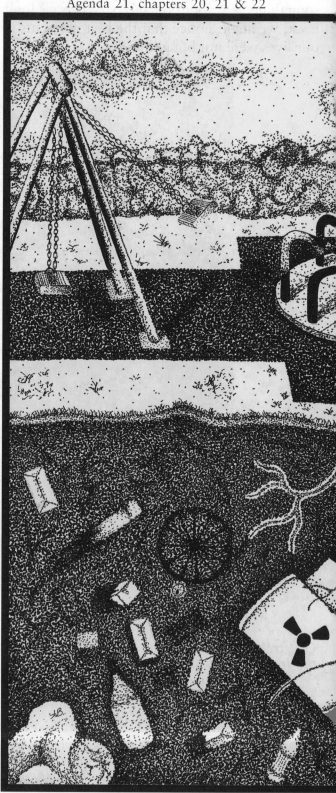

Unsustainable consumption, particularly in industrialized nations, is increasing the amount and variety of wastes. Quantities could increase four to fivefold by the year 2025.

Agenda 21, chapters 20, 21 & 22

During the race for progress, most of us forgot to collect the stuff we dropped along the way. That's the reality which is now catching up with us. It's like a huge snake that has been slowly coiling itself around us. Now it's beginning to hurt. We've been producing more and more waste including chemicals and nuclear material that will hang around and be dangerous for hundreds, even thousands, of years. It's time to panic - and to act! Soon there will be no more room for these mountains of rubbish.

Agenda 21 devotes three chapters to this problem: first it looks at solid waste - sewage, household garbage. Second at hazardous waste, poisonous stuff, lethal to us and to our environment. Lastly, at nuclear waste that comes from nuclear power stations and bomb factories.

SOLID WASTE
This is set to increase four to five times by 2025. In developing countries, less than 10% of human sewage is treated. If we do nothing to change this, by 2025 the planet will be engulfed in a mountain of human manure!

My mother weeps
I was proud to call her my mother
           - today it's not the same.
I smash the sewage right into her face
Sorry if I hurt her spirit, her lovely taste
She throws a glance - there's nothing new
Just the same old dirty view. She weeps
           - and weeps, seeing those solids lay
Her rivers flowing all turned grey
And her sons dying for there's no other way.
           Dharna Gupta, 13, India

HAZARDOUS WASTE

The industrial revolution has changed life in developed countries from a struggle of survival to the complex high-tech experience it is today. Industry works with increasing speed to fulfill our various needs.

The dark side of this is all the poisonous leftovers nobody seems to have knowledge, interest or money to treat. Each year, 260 million tons of hazardous waste is produced in the USA - many times that in the rest of the world. Worst, poor countries have become dumping grounds for the hazardous waste of rich nations. Out of sight, out of mind!

NUCLEAR WASTE

Our invisible gift to future generations! Every year, tons and tons of it are produced and trucked across industrialized countries. No new nuclear power stations are being built, but the problem of several hundred existing ones remains.

There is no method of storage that is guaranteed to be safe in an earthquake. By the year 2000, there'll be 100,000 truck loads of radioactive waste stored in Great Britain alone! This is a problem our generation will have to face and one that will still be around for our great, great, great grandchildren.

Emily Monaghan, 17, UK

TOXIC CHEMICALS

Chemicals are a vital part of our modern world used in virtually every industry and human process. Trouble is, many of them are "toxic" or poisonous. Toxic chemicals that are banned in rich countries are transported and illegally dumped in poor countries which do not have the capacity to deal with them. There is currently no global agreement on trade in toxic chemicals.

Agenda 21, Chapter 19

Invisible Death *Adam Bellis, 17, UK*

OPERATION CLEANUP

Prevent or minimize the generation of waste. This should be part of an overall cleaner production approach; by 2010, all countries should have national plans for waste management.

Agenda 21, chapters 20 & 22

There is a clear solution to the waste problem: waste should not be produced in the first place. We've got used to waste as an inevitable fact of life but in fact waste is always a big mistake. Industry can and should introduce ways of making things without producing waste.

" *One of the interesting things happening on human settlements, is some wonderful work that has been done on the development of the indigenous materials for housing. We're actually creating housing materials from waste. This is being done in a number of countries - bricks made from waste are actually produced in different countries so we're creating new industries, jobs and so on as well as using up waste.*

Elizabeth Dowdeswell, Under-Secretary-General
UNEP/HABITAT

"

WHAT CAN WE DO?

Do not create waste. Buy only things that you really need and things that last. When you can't make use of them any more, recycle or find another person who needs them.

Compost all your household waste; use a compost toilet to dispose of your sewage. Don't buy products that are wrapped in unnecessary, cute covers.

The most important thing is to pressure industry to move on to waste-free processes. Try to find out which companies are wasting what and let it influence your shopping decisions. Then boycott their products. When enough of us do that, they will have to change their ways.

AGENDA 21 SAYS:

• Reduce waste, recycle and tax packaging materials.
• Require that industry adopt cleaner production methods.
• Developed countries: promote the transfer of low-waste production methods to developing countries.
• Give the people the right to know the risks of chemicals they are exposed to.
• Immediately clean up contaminated areas and give help to their inhabitants.
• Make polluters pay cleanup costs.
• Ensure that the military disposes of their hazardous waste properly.
• Ban illegal export of hazardous waste to countries not equipped to deal with it.
• Minimize creation of radioactive waste.

Nnammonso B. Asuquo, Nigeria

EXPLOSION AT KLONG TOEY, 1991

One Saturday afternoon in March an unusual billowing cloud of smoke was seen hovering in the air. We all knew that Bangkok was polluted, but we never thought that it was that bad. There were chemicals in the air, in exposed food and water and in the blood of the residents of these areas.

The accident probably started when containers of phosporus ignited spontaneously in front of a warehouse, producing an intense fire which quickly consumed several warehouses.

It has left behind many serious problems - complaints of itchy skin, rashes, wounds that took place at the time and have never healed; pregnant women whose babies have died in the womb. To make matters worse many of the people fell ill.

The residents of the Klong Toey area are not aware how serious and toxic the explosion was. Although many were offered other temporary housing they preferred to remain where they were. Those whose homes were destroyed wanted to rebuild their shacks over the burnt and contaminated area.

After the explosion, jerrycans, drums and plastic bags containing lethal chemicals, acids that survived the fire were stacked all over the surrounding areas. Despite warnings on the containers - to keep these materials in cool temperatures, out of direct sunlight - they were left unprotected, directly in the sun. The result was fire. Warnings about not using these cans to extinguish fire were totally ignored.

Another problem was that many large amounts of chemicals stored in Klong Toey ports were unlabelled. More than 50 % of chemical cargo kept in the Port Authority of Thailand warehouses were moved out of the Klong Toey port area during the following weeks. Nobody knows where they went.

It seems to me, that government officials in Bangkok don't want to take responsibility for such problems when they occur. The result is confusion about "it's someone else's responsibility." Many people knew the chemicals were being stored under wrong conditions but because of this "May-pen-rai" (never mind) attitude, Thai residents suffered. We hope that the Thai government learnt a lesson from this horrible experience. In the short term they need to look at relocation and housing assistance for the people who lived in the Klong Toey area. The government could move the people out of Bangkok to start a housing program on less expensive land. They could then provide free transportation for their jobs in the city. They have started to clean up the Klong Toey slum, although this is more due to pressure from citizens that government efficiency.

For the future, the government must prevent this sort of problem happening again. Inexpensive health care and housing programs need to be started for the poor, possibly through taxes and donations. There should also be better enviromental education for the whole community through schools, newspapers and television. There is a TV program once a week which informs people of the enviromental problems being faced in Thailand. This is the step in the right direction.

Lalana Panijpan, 18, Thailand

Ivan Sekulovic, 17, Serbia

SOIL RUNNING OUT

*There's only so much land in our world.
Expanding human requirements are increasing
pressures on it, creating competition and conflicts.*

Agenda 21, chapter 12

As our consumption, wants and needs increase, more land is needed to feed our growing numbers. If cheap and careless farming methods are used, the land gets less fertile. It can turn into deserts. At best, it becomes degraded and unproductive. Soil and land are under heavy stress today. With the large increases in population expected, every scrap of land has to be looked after very carefully.

Problem of Storage

*I trod the bush track daily
With my hoe and matchet on my shoulder
Coming home with my harvest
I have no good place to store it
But to increase the heap of refuse
Behind my house.
The scorching sun burns my back mercilessly
Sweat and rain soak my clothes
The drudgery of toil weighs heavily on me
I have found no solution; I have no alternative but to
toil in sweat and pain
For the little I eat.*

Mary Edet, 15, Nigeria

WINDBREAKS
Modern farmers tend to pull down the hedgerows which enable them to seed more land and drive bigger machinery across their farms. This raises the productivity but only for a short time. In the long run, it degrades the land. Also, hedges are home to all sorts of wild life and flowers which die when their hedgerow homes are destroyed. Without the hedges as windbreaks, much of the fertile soil blows away.

Agata Pawlat, 17, Poland

SCIENCE FAILED
Between 1950 and 1980, the world produced more and more food each year. In the 1980's the increase stopped. In some areas we produce less food. Scientists have developed new cereals which ripen earlier and produce more grain. But these crops need fertilizer and pesticides but pesticides kill more than just pests. They kill the bugs that keep the land healthy. Now science, which has helped double and re-double grain yields through the 50's and 60's, is running out of new ideas. So how will we feed our extra billions?

Hana Barackova, 13, Czech Republic

Take one last look
Take a seat under a tree
and let the stillness envelop you.
Let the liana softly stroke your hair
as you watch patches of sun light
dancing on the fallen leaves
Listen carefully and you will hear
the gurgling of a near by stream,
the chat of monkeys
in the branches above you.
Look carefully you will see
the verdant green of
young shoots
straining towards
the sun light
you will notice the bright
splashes of tiny red and
yellow flowers.
Look long and hard,
For you will want
to be able to remember
and describe this to your
grandchildren
when you return
many years from now
and find only a bare,
arid desert.
Aditi Charda, Tanzania

Ekaterina Kotova, 15, Russia

Global warming
causes evaporation
from soils and reduces
crop yields.

DESERTIFICATION
In many places, soil has lost its natural
goodness because farmers have over-used it,
ploughing it year after year for their crops.
This sucks the goodness out of the soil until
eventually it becomes like dust and is blown
away by wind or washed away by rain.

SALINIZATION
Salinization happens when irrigation water
evaporates and leaves behind salts which
harden into a rock hard surface. This makes
land impossible to plough. Salinization is
damaging 7% of the worlds croplands.

Agata Pawlat, 17, Poland

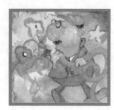

HAPPY FARMERS

The priority must be to maintain and improve the capacity of agricultural lands to support an expanding population.

Agenda 21, chapter 14

To plan the way we use our precious land, we must include everyone in the planning - indigenous people, women, young people, scientists and experts in rural development. Agenda 21 urges greater conservation, greater sharing of information, but it doesn't touch on the all important areas of land ownership. Without firm control of their land, no farmer is going to be entirely happy.

LESS MEAT

Soil degradation is sometimes caused by overgrazing. In the USA, 85% of the soil lost is directly attributed to the creation of livestock for consumption. In addition, 50% of the freshwater resources is used to irrigate pasture and food crops for cattle. Switching to a vegetarian or reduced meat diet would definitely bring environmental advantages.

Agata Pawlat, 17, Poland

ORGANIC FARMING

There is a growing number of farmers who are concerned about the effects of chemicals on the environment and who have turned to organic methods. They use natural compost and animal manure to fertilize their fields. These farmers choose crop rotation instead of growing the same thing on the same field every year. So they don't wear out the soil or let the numbers of pests which attack a particular crop build up. They don't use chemical sprays but instead increase the natural resistance of their crops and animals to pests and diseases.

Naturally there are drawbacks: it takes at least two years before the land can be cured of all the chemicals that have been poured into it. In those years, the farmer will earn very little. Also, organic farming may need more hand labour, more workers and thus be more expensive to produce. For these and other reasons, there are still very few organic farmers about.

Kerala

Dump the fertilizers. Damn the pesticides. Sow what you want. Leave the weeds alone and leave the rest to nature. This is exactly what M.P George of Kerala, India has done. The results are astounding. The soil which was dying due to the increasing use of fertilizers and pesticides began to rejuvenate. The earthworms came back. The life giving microbes thrived. Spiders once again made the farm their home, gobbling up pests. The soil became rich in humus. Even the weeds contribute to it. After five years of such farming, his land has become a gold-mine.

Rekha Menon, 14, India

Xu Xi, 13, China

The Impossible becomes Possible
We should work and produce enough food
Sustaining this land. feeding the people;
But how will this be done?
To sit on the fence will bring no change,
With hatred - impossible
With cheating - impossible
But with love and unity
The impossible becomes possible.

Uduak Enefiok, 15, Nigeria

AGENDA 21 SAYS:
• Bring together everyone who works on the land for planning meetings: local farmers, women, managers, business-people, local officials, sales agents, scientists, government officials.
• Make laws to end the devastation of land by mining (*polluter pays principle*).
• Governments must provide advice to farmers on environmentally friendly fertilizers.
• All farmers must be educated in methods of preserving topsoil.
• Encourage farmers to switch to renewable energy sources.
• Tell farmers about the problem of ultra-violet rays reaching their crops; research ways to minimise the effects of loss of the ozone layer and global warming.
• Raise people's awareness through education and campaigns.

LIVING ON THE EDGE

A growing number of cities are showing symptoms of the global environment and development crisis, ranging from air pollution to homeless street dwellers.

Agenda 21, chapter 7

Cities have always been the centre of hustle and bustle. It made work much easier because everything was in one place. But we got other problems. Cities kept on growing and growing, to the point of not being able to cope. People flooded in making what is called "Mega Cities"- ones with more than 10 million people. By the year 2000, there will be more than 25 Mega Cities and most of them are large, over-crowded, over-built, polluted, creaking catastrophies...

LIFE IN THE BIG CITY

Another gray morning in New York City. As I look up, I see nothing but a blanket that prevents sun from shining. I reach the corner of the street and see a whirlpool of garbage on the pavement.

On my bike now cycling through the busy streets of midtown. I get caught behind the bus with rows of cars either side. I tuck my head into my shirt so as not to inhale fumes coming from every direction.

On my way home, I go through Central Park, safe heaven in this concrete town. Yet even in its deepest corner, you can't escape the famous skyline standing high and overpowering against a mauve sky.

Another gray evening in New York City.
Analia, 17, USA

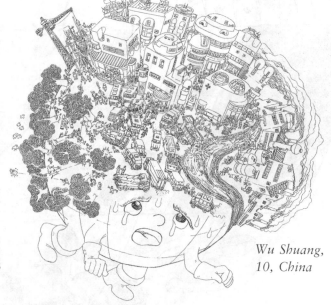

Wu Shuang, 10, China

P. Ponnamperuma, 17, Sri Lanka

Cities
In an ancient light
of stars,
the solid city of
concrete,
suddenly becomes
a gaping wound,
bleeding
of a silent melody,
of a million
beating hearts.
Stella Parland, 19, Finland

Istanbul

The natural habitats in and around Istanbul haven't changed since the last ice-age. They are rich in wildlife with some species which cannot be found in any other part of the Earth. But now this historic city of 11 million inhabitants is in danger. Already a mega city, it's population will double by the year 2025 - something I can't imagine without terror! Shanty towns are springing up everywhere, uncontrolled and illegal. They pollute drinking water and endanger the community. Big construction projects destroy the environment because they are not well planned. DKHD, Natural life Protection Fund has started a Green Zone project to protect the natural habitats.

Birce Boga, 17, Turkiye (Turkey)

MY HOUSE

Governments should see that the homeless get access to land, credit and low-cost building materials. Agenda 21, chapter 7

Cities must be planned better. "Better" means in an environmentaly-friendly way. City public transportation should be cheap and well organ- ized. City sewage should be recycled and treated for use in fertilization. Household rubbish should be recycled into compost then used for parks and green spaces. Most important are strict city limits and prevention of uncontrolled expansion.

J. Claude Bigirimana, 17, Burundi

CASE STUDY 21

Eco-community

If you were to create a town for 12,000 people that was a model of eco-responsibility, what would it be like?
Bamberton in Canada tries to be the answer. Every house is eco-efficient; 85% of waste is recycled, much of it into compost to feed local fruit trees in parks (called edible landscaping!)
Local shops, schools and businesses allow people to use cars less; roads give way to big old trees, bending round them creating twisting streets, slowing traffic; houses are laid out to encourage conversations and build community. Once built, a town may last a thousand years. More than anyone else, town builders are accountable to future generations and their unspoken needs. *Guy Dauncey, quoted by In Context magazine*

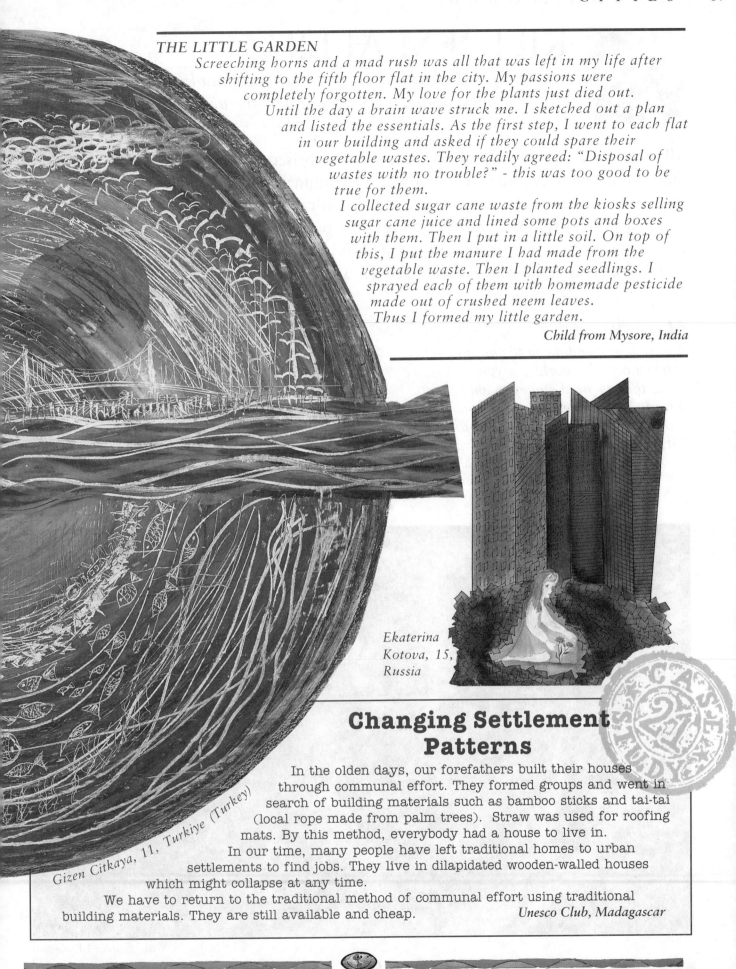

THE LITTLE GARDEN

Screeching horns and a mad rush was all that was left in my life after shifting to the fifth floor flat in the city. My passions were completely forgotten. My love for the plants just died out.

Until the day a brain wave struck me. I sketched out a plan and listed the essentials. As the first step, I went to each flat in our building and asked if they could spare their vegetable wastes. They readily agreed: "Disposal of wastes with no trouble?" - this was too good to be true for them.

I collected sugar cane waste from the kiosks selling sugar cane juice and lined some pots and boxes with them. Then I put in a little soil. On top of this, I put the manure I had made from the vegetable waste. Then I planted seedlings. I sprayed each of them with homemade pesticide made out of crushed neem leaves.

Thus I formed my little garden.

Child from Mysore, India

Ekaterina Kotova, 15, Russia

Gizen Citkaya, 11, Turkiye (Turkey)

Changing Settlement Patterns

In the olden days, our forefathers built their houses through communal effort. They formed groups and went in search of building materials such as bamboo sticks and tai-tai (local rope made from palm trees). Straw was used for roofing mats. By this method, everybody had a house to live in.

In our time, many people have left traditional homes to urban settlements to find jobs. They live in dilapidated wooden-walled houses which might collapse at any time.

We have to return to the traditional method of communal effort using traditional building materials. They are still available and cheap.

Unesco Club, Madagascar

KILL 'EM ALL!!

Warfare is inherently destructive of sustainable development, so effective laws, respected by all states are needed...

Rio Declaration, Principle 24

All of us who took part in this exercise were surprised by one thing: there's nothing in Agenda 21 about war and militarism! Agenda 21 can never happen without peace. So why doesn't it get a mention? One reason was that the Gulf War was going on as the Agenda was being written: no government wanted to have limits placed on its ability to make war. Another reason was money.

> *We are overspending on the means destruction. The world is saying - "Yes, we know that we need money to implement Agenda 21 and we know it's a small proportion of what we spend on the military but we cannot see a way to do it ...*
>
> Sir Shridath Ramphal, Co-chair,
> Commission on Global Governance

THE WASTE OF WAR

The military wastes lives, wastes the time of some of our best engineers and scientists, and wastes huge amounts of money - close to a trillion dollars a year! With the end of the Cold War, that figure is declining but it is still far too high. The military also wastes the environment: according to the Worldwatch Institute, the military is "the single biggest polluter on earth." Worst of all, war wastes childhood.

My Name is War   *Boris, 14, Russia*

Peace is not just the absence of war -

PEACE IS A STATE OF MIND

You cannot destroy an enemy by shooting him. That only creates more enemies. The only way to destroy an enemy is to make him your friend.
Peace Child, 1992

There MUST be something we can do! Kids have in the past helped to resolve conflict: youth exchanges helped heal French/German relations after World War II. Samantha Smith's letter to the Russian leader in 1983, triggered events which helped change US and Soviet peoples' feelings about each other. Children must stand up to their parents and tell them war is crazy. It has to stop! If we don't, it is we who are called up to fight.

SNAPSHOTS FROM A WAR

There's a war going on in my country. Nobody believed it was happening. We were expecting it to stop any day. It was insane: nobody wanted it. Soon it spread to Bosnia. Now there's so much pain and hatred around it's hard to think. The ones who suffer the most are children. They're losing their parents, families, friends - childhood. I have seen a gray-haired 13 year old refugee. I didn't dare look into his eyes. These children are going to grow up soon. What can we expect from them? This is the most scary thought for me. *A child from Croatia*

Ivan Sekulovic, 17, Serbia

My Name is Peace *Ekaterina Kotova, 15, Russia*

" *We can't stop this war right now but we won't let it go on in our hearts. We must be responsible enough to be able to forgive.*
Daniela, 19, Croatia "

He and she are brother and sister. He is a little older and he cares about his sister because there is nobody else to do it. Their parents got killed in war. Also their grandmother, grandfather, uncle and... the list is too long. It all happened suddenly like a short summer storm: some bad people taked their land but leaved them alive - alone, hungry and very scared. The only strength they find now is from their joint embrace. They want to wake up and find that it is all just a bad dream after which their mother will welcome them with a tender lullaby and send them to a better dream. The two of them are still waiting. *A child from Serbia*

PART III

MAKING IT HAPPEN
WHO'S GOING TO DO ALL THIS?

WHO'S THE BOSS?

Agenda 21 reflects a global consensus at the highest level. Its successful implementation is first and foremost the responsibility of governments....

Agenda 21, Preamble

Governments lead our countries. They wrote Agenda 21. They have the money to make it happen but, with most, the energy generated by Rio is already slipping. Some one has to check to see they are keeping their promises.

GOVERNMENTS ARE TOPS

What are the words that come up most often in Agenda 21? We did a word count on the computer to find out how often certain words are used. This is what we came up with:

Hit Words of Agenda 21:

10.	Disabled	6
9.	Children	66
8.	Youth	80
7.	Indigenous people	162
6.	Education	249
5.	Women	272
4.	Training	368
3.	Cooperation	416
2.	Research	421
1.	Government	**1107**

> **AGENDA 21 SAYS:**
>
> Governments must:
> • Develop National Agenda 21s to make sure that new laws aren't just good for the economy but for people and the environment as well.
> • Provide technical support to countries who can't enforce environmental laws.
> • Tax products that aren't ecologically friendly so that people will buy those products that don't harm the environment.
> • Introduce environmental accounting: governments and businesses must stop thinking of natural resources as free sources of profit. For example, they must include the cost of regrowing a forest in the "cost" side of their accounts.

Environmental Accounting

Anna Grzybowska, 16, Poland

UN-STOPPABLE

The United Nations is uniquely placed to help governments achieve the objectives of Agenda 21. The UN itself should rebuild and revitalize itself around these goals.

Agenda 21, chapters 37 & 38

Since Rio, the UN has kept its promise to set up offices to help governments implement Agenda 21. It has worked to find ways to close the gap between the rich and poor nations.

Christopher Weil, 18, Germany

Third World's Lament
The First World has had its fun
The Third World's just begun
But fluorocarbons from the fridge
Make ozone holes we cannot bridge
So poverty must be our lot
And development, it seems, must stop.

The First World now has made its gold
With grand new plans it makes so bold
Fudging figures to give skewed statistics
(Developed folk are adept at these antics!)
They tell us:
"Rice fields pollute more than our cars!"
So pressure is put on poor countries like ours
For decades of indulgence, they pay no price,
But in such matters, we have no rights.
Loans are witheld;
Hard bargains are driven.
With backs against the wall,
We toe the line.
The First World goes all out for their kill
And the poorer nations become poorer still.
A change of heart must take place
If the poorer world is to see better days.
Rekha Menon, 14, India

SHARING INFORMATION

The UN is the coordinating force in making Agenda 21 a reality. It has already created an information network on sustainable development. It will also hold a special session no later than 1997 to review progress.

CAPACITY BUILDING

The increasing gap between the differing worlds of the rich and the poor is clear throughout Agenda 21. For example, the North has twice as much university education, 50% more scientists and technicians, more radios, more computers, four times as many telephones - the list is endless.

Bridging of this gap, according to Agenda 21, is called capacity building. This basically means providing people with education and local services so that they can understand and carry out sustainable development. To make this possible UNDP has started Capacity 21, a training programme, operating at a local level.

Michael Kanyako, 22, Sierra Leone

WE'RE IN IT TOGETHER

Fundamental to the achievement of sustainable development is broad public participation by all major social groups.

Agenda 21, chapters 23, 24, 26, 27, 29, 30 & 32

Agenda 21 is mainly targeted at our governments but that doesn't mean that the rest of us are not involved. We all know that the Agenda is not going to happen unless every group and person in society feels responsible for putting it into effect. Agenda 21 mentions nine major groups and how they should cooperate with the government.

1. WOMEN

Women make up over half of the world's population. This alone should make them one of the most powerful groups in society. Still in many countries, most women haven't got access to even the most elementary schooling or the possibility to work outside their home, and millions of women are physically abused every day.

66

In Sierra Leone, only a quarter of the women get primary schooling. It's better in the cities, but out in the villages a woman's only duty is to cook for the man and care for the children. She has no role in decision-making, not even concerning her family or herself.

Sheku Kamara, 19, Sierra Leone

99

AGENDA 21 SAYS:
Have more women decision-makers, planners, scientists! Governments should:
• Set up education programmes so all women can learn to read and write.
• Make sure women in developing countries have rights to own land and get credit from banks.
• Make women aware of the environmental consequences of what they buy through eco-labelling, especially in rich countries.
• Help set up child care so more women can go to work.
• Do everything possible to stop violence against women.

India

It's rather surprising in a place like India to find an actual matriarchal society. In most of India it seems that men have a hold on everything, but in Lakshwadeep and Kerala in Southern India it's the woman who is boss. In the rest of India the girl is supposed to give dowry to the bridegroom, but here the bridegroom gives a dowry to the girl. In Lakshwadeep and Kerala women are better educated and as well as taking care of their homes, they are the breadwinners of the family. They keep accounts of family expenditure, run the shops and are generally responsible for running the community.

Rekha Menon, 14, India

2. NON-GOVERNMENTAL ORGANIZATIONS

Non-Governmental Organisations (NGOs) are charities and pressure groups formed by ordinary people, independent of governments and political parties, eg Greenpeace, World Wild Life Fund and Amnesty International. They have a wealth of expertise and energy vital to the making the agenda work. We hope that many will work with young people on the Rescue Mission.

AGENDA 21 SAYS:

• Get close communication between governments and NGOs.
• Cooperation between NGOs themselves should be increased.
• UN agencies should support NGOs.
• Freedom for NGOs to say things and promote ideas that governments and industry might not like must be guaranteed.

GREENPEACE   PEACE CHILD   WWF   The Centre for Our Common Future

3. TRADE UNIONS

The goal of sustainable development is to provide jobs for everyone in a safe, clean environment. Trade unions have organized radical changes in workers' conditions.

AGENDA 21 SAYS:

• Workers should take part in all decisions, cooperating with both employers and governments.
• Trade unions should promote worker education and training in work health and safety.

4. BUSINESS

Business plays a very important role in any kind of development. A large part of conservation, resource use, waste reduction, rights of workers, etc. lies in the hands of the businessmen!

AGENDA 21 SAYS:

• Environmental management should be given a lot of importance and national business councils should be set up for that purpose.
• Measures should be taken to reduce the industry's impact on the environment and develop cleaner production methods.

Sebastian & Victor, Chile

Christopher Weil, 18, Germany

5. INDIGENOUS PEOPLE

Indigenous people know their land better than anyone. As civilization advances, it threatens to destroy them and their knowledge. They held a meeting in Rio where they declared: "We walk to the future in the footprints of our ancestors which are permanently etched on our lands."

AGENDA 21 SAYS :

Governments should:
• Let indigenous people take an active part in all political decisions affecting them and their land.
• Respect and protect the property and culture of indigenous people.

From the smallest to the largest living being, from the air, the land and the mountains, the creator has placed us, the indigenous peoples, upon our Mother Earth.
Indigenous Peoples Declaration, Rio de Janeiro, June '92

6. FARMERS

Indigenous people, rural dwellers and family farmers are the actual caretakers of much of the world's resources: they are directly in touch with the environment. Agriculture occupies a third of the world's land surface and is a central activity for much of the world's population. This is why farmers have a chapter to themselves in the Agenda.

AGENDA 21 SAYS:

• Give more responsibility to farmers.
• Develop farming practices and technologies that are safe for the environment.
• Farmers should share knowledge on conservation of natural resources.
• Bring ecology into agricultural training.
• Prices of agricultural products need to reflect environmental costs.

Michael Kanyako, 22, Sierra Leone

7. Children and Youth, see pages 77-91
8. Local Authorities, see opposite page
9. Science and Technology, see page 70

LOCAL POLITICS

Local authorities, as the level of government closest to people, have a vital role in educating and mobilizing the public to get behind the goals of Agenda 21.

Agenda 21, chapter 28

Every local authority should prepare a Local Agenda 21 to link the interests of local people in business, public services and ordinary citizens.

AGENDA 21 SAYS:

• Local governments should draw up their own Agenda 21s to reshape the policies, laws and regulations of their districts.

• Local governments should work with international organizations and with each other to gain new ideas.

• By 1994, local governments should be linked at an international level.

• By 1996, each local authority must present their local Agenda 21.

England's Local Agenda

In Hertfordshire, England where we edited this book, we decided to check out how the local government was getting on preparing its Local Agenda 21. The conclusion was they were doing pretty well: they have set up a way to talk to all interested groups in the county: the Herts Environmental Forum. They have also done a complete environmental audit and forecast.

Doing this, they found that the number of private cars was set to double in the next 30 years and public transport had fallen by 40% in 20 years! People in Hertfordshire just like to use their cars. "This is our biggest challenge," says Peter Jackson, the environmental officer. "We can't continue to build new roads all over our county. We're looking at different ways to reduce private car use. By the year 2000, we are required by law to recycle 25% of the county's domestic waste. People here haven't caught on yet. In one town, some returned the recycling bins we provided."

So how do you get people to change their dangerous habits? Jackson says: "The answer is a massive education scheme. Children can really help to educate their parents. They must tell them to use their cars less and compost and recycle more. Only in this way is Hertfordshire going to meet its Local Agenda 21 targets."

Anuragini Nagar, 19, India

Hertfordshire
COUNTY COUNCIL

APPLIANCE OF SCIENCE

Scientists and technologists have special responsibilities to search for knowledge and to help protect the biosphere.

Agenda 21, chapters 31, 34 & 35

Science and technology are very important in Agenda 21. The key point made is that the scientists and decision-makers should share information. This should also be encouraged between the north and the south.

Biotechnology

Tan Mei Hong, Malaysia

RESEARCH

Human needs and the environment are changing fast - scientists can help by investigating these changes.

SHARING TECHNOLOGY

As pollution spreads over borders it is important that all countries have environmentally safe technologies. The problem is that it is expensive to create good technology. But, in the long-term, isn't it cheaper for companies or nations to give away their eco-technology than to have poor countries go on polluting?

BIOTECHNOLOGY

Biotechnology is changing the genetics of a species or combining two species to make a new one. It tries to improve human health, agriculture and industry, for example, by creating crops that grow with little water. Most importantly, biotechnology could help to repair the damage we have already done to the environment. But we can never be sure of the results of our experiments (remember *Jurassic Park!*) We must be careful when playing with nature.

WHY TRANSFER TECHNOLOGY?

Tony and Herman were neighbors. Herman is very bright - an inventor. Tony is not so bright - he earns a living by selling carrots. Herman invents a gadget to clean up his home called a Techno Recycle Assistance Service wHat ChamacAllit Network - or TRASH CAN for short. This invention takes all kinds of junk and turns them in to fertilizers. Herman sells his gadget to rich people not to poor people *like Tony. Junk builds up in Tony's backyard until soon it starts to overflow into neighbor Herman's backyard. One day, in desperation, Herman decides to give Tony a TRASH CAN. And an amazing thing happens: not only does he get rid of the junk, Tony gets more carrots and eventually pays Herman back. The neighbors live happily and peacefully ever after.*

William Chung, Thailand

Agata Pawlat, 17, Poland

WHAT PRICE?

Very large investments are needed to implement the huge sustainable development programmes of Agenda 21.

Agenda 21, chapter 33

Until recently we were taking things like clean drinking water, forests and other natural resources for granted. But now we must realize that these things are no longer freely available to all. We will have to pay for keeping our environment clean and repairing the damage done.

TOTAL COST OF AGENDA 21?
$600,000,000,000!

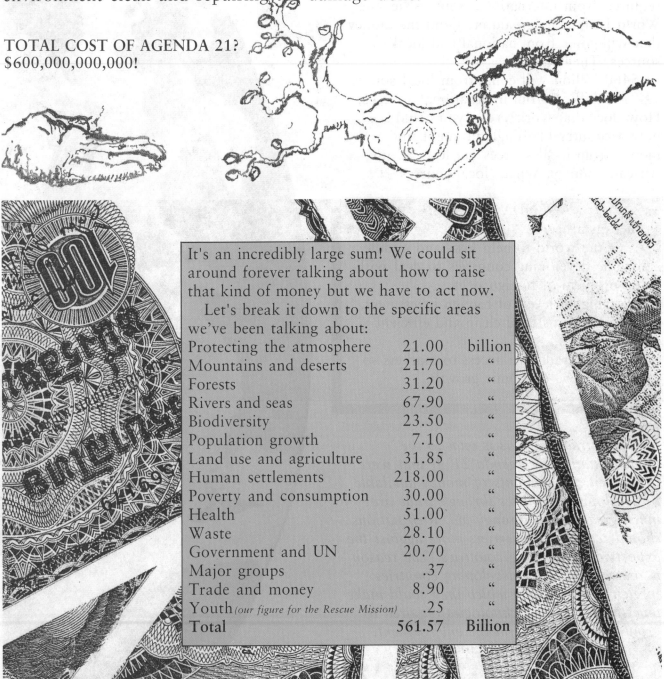

It's an incredibly large sum! We could sit around forever talking about how to raise that kind of money but we have to act now.
Let's break it down to the specific areas we've been talking about:

Protecting the atmosphere	21.00	billion
Mountains and deserts	21.70	"
Forests	31.20	"
Rivers and seas	67.90	"
Biodiversity	23.50	"
Population growth	7.10	"
Land use and agriculture	31.85	"
Human settlements	218.00	"
Poverty and consumption	30.00	"
Health	51.00	"
Waste	28.10	"
Government and UN	20.70	"
Major groups	.37	"
Trade and money	8.90	"
Youth *(our figure for the Rescue Mission)*	.25	"
Total	561.57	Billion

MONEY DOESN'T GROW ON TREES

Without money, none of the grand ideas of Agenda 21 can get done. It will remain a dream - a tempting wish list.

WHERE IS THE MONEY GOING TO COME FROM?

In Agenda 21, they separate out the money required from international sources (ie. the World Bank, foreign aid etc.) and the money that will come from national and local sources. They calculate:

• $460 billion will come from local sources
• $140 billion from international sources.

How does that work? Yes - you could see how a country like England might find money from local sources but look at any African country. What "local sources"?!

AGENDA 21 SAYS:

There is a need -
• For the world to help low- and middle income developing countries to deal with the problem of foreign debt.
• For higher levels of foreign investment.
• For the transfer of clean and efficient technologies.
• For free trade and access to markets so as to achieve economic growth.

Reducing trade barriers is vital to the implementation of Agenda 21. If that were to happen, the amounts of money available to developing countries through trade are much greater than through aid. Rich nations should reduce their barriers more against the exports of developing countries. The reason is that exports earn developing countries foreign currency with which they could make investments in the technologies required to grow fast and not harm the environment.

Andrew Steer, World Bank

Developing nations need free trade and access to markets in order to achieve the economic growth that will enable them to grow in a sustainable way.

Agenda 21, chapter 33

Tina Tuohi, Finland

MONEY FOR NOTHING

The world still sticks to the old Roman maxim: *si vis pacem, para bellum*. If you want peace, prepare for war. We still do! Whatever the situation, there is always enough money for a Gulf War or nuclear missiles. Why is there never enough to give us all a respectable living? Military spending is far more than is needed for Agenda 21.

> ### AGENDA 21 SAYS:
> • Funds could be raised by reallocating resources now committed to the military.

POLLUTER PAYS PRINCIPLE

Those who pollute should pay for the damage they cause to the environment through green taxes. These will encourage polluters to invest in cleaner technology. In the meantime, the money raised can be spent on transferring more safe, clean technology to developing countries.

THE RIGHT PRIORITIES

The biggest problems don't need so much money. UNICEF calculates an additional 25 billion dollars a year could -
  • Control major childhood diseases
  • Halve the number of starving children
  • Bring clean water to all communities
  • Bring primary education to all children
  • Make population programmes and
      family planning universally available.
At the same time -
  • America spends $31 billion on beer
      every year
  • Europe spends $50 billion on cigarettes
  • Hong Kong's new airport will cost $23
      billion
So for the cost of a new airport or half what the Europeans spend giving themselves cancer with cigarettes, we could give a far better life to all people living on this Earth!

TO WANT + TO KNOW = TO ACT

Make environment and development education available to people of all ages.

Agenda 21, chapter 36

Lack of education is one of the biggest obstacles to development. If people don't know what things are harmful to the environment, how can they respect it? Many people in the world don't even know how to read or write. All people, both adults and kids, have to get primary schooling before they can be taught about environment and development.

The Need of Education

Imagine how dreary life would have been,
Living in ignorance and monotony,
Staring at the everyday life roll by—
Without a care.........
Writing scribbles on the dead sand,
While glancing at the once brilliant horizon.

Someone wants to break the spell,
Their inability to express strong feelings held back
for so long, the inability to fight for their rights
and get what they longed for.
Dust and steam torment the lonely man,
But to achieve his goal, he must fight.

But when he comes back, he shall be victorious;
And will bring a thought, an intelligent teacher,
To bring a colorful, bright rainbow to lighten the way;
To change our futures, for the better...
To help us live.

Portia Villanueva, 11, Philippines

"

I personally think if women are given a real education they will strive hard to do their very best. For instance, if I had no education I wouldn't have had the opportunity to attend the Editorial Meeting of the Children's Edition of Agenda 21 and get the book published for a better future.   Mary Edet, 15, Nigeria

"

AGENDA 21 SAYS:
• Make basic education available to as many people as possible.
• Set up training programmes on sustainable development.
• Promote awareness on environment, and make use of media and the entertainment industry.
• Promote the knowledge of indigenous people.
• Create partnerships with companies in the developing countries to teach environmental management.

Chamsai Menasveta, 17, Thailand

José Luis Bayer, Chile

PART IV

YOUNG PEOPLE

OUR ROLE

IDEAS AND ENERGY

What can we do? So many people ask this question, we almost expect the answer, "Nothing." Not true! - in editing this book, we found we're all doing something positive. We're not unusual: millions of kids are doing many different things already. This is us!

Debbie, 16, England: I go to an incredibly active school. Every kid plants an acorn when they arrive. We have a sister school in Kenya to which we send computers and books; they send us craftwork which we sell.

Uli, 18, Germany: I started ecological activities when I was president of my Student Council - organizing the recycling of paper, collections, information boards etc. I also push ecoissues in the European Youth Parliament.

Hemara, 18, Switzerland: I started an ecological group at my school. We organize awareness and action campaigns. The Rescue Mission has shown me how inseparable environment and development concerns are, an emphasis I'd like to bring to the group.

Dann, 22, USA: I'm an actor. I perform with a theater group called Klub Tribe which does plays on social and environmental issues. We rehearse and perform every week-end. I tour with the group throughout the States and individually with Peace Child Internationional.

Ronnie, 19, USA: I am an environmental and political play-wright. I always promote a green line in speeches and debates but there is not much enthusiasm or knowledge. Personally, the Rescue Mission is important because it will help me begin my own movement at home.

Arancha, 19, Spain: Environment has never been a topic in my school, nor development! It is just starting here, and the Rescue Mission is the push we really need. I will be talking to my Education minister to get it into the curriculum.

Tanya, 19, Italy: I am working with the press, politicians and school officials to get a session of the European Youth Parliament in Milan. It's hard work! I think the Rescue Mission will enhance the role of the youth.

Viola, 12, Italy: I try to keep my environment clean. The children of our school wrote to the mayor to ask for recycling facilities to be installed on campus - they were provided. The Rescue Mission will help us do more.

Sheku and Michael, 20 & 22, Sierra Leone: We organize an eco-clean up day every month, and have symposia to improve the situation of women in our society. It's a great time in our country: our new President is 24 years old and he's hard-working. We want to have a campaign to teach everybody to read and write.

José Luis & Victoriano, 25 & 15, Chile: We took part in the Latin American Encounter on Ecology - José designed the poster and all the art work and cartoons for this. As a result the group "Academia de Ciencias" of "San Juan Evangelista School" started work on the Agenda 21 project. We plan to spread the Rescue Mission throughout Latin America.

Mary, 15, Nigeria: We have an Environment Conservation and Preservation Club which arose out of our work on Agenda 21. We take care of the school environment, go to villages etc. We will strongly promote Rescue Mission.

Mia, 19, Finland: I do volunteer work in a shop that sells Third World products. The money goes to the people who make the goods, not to middle-men. We also pressure the government about their policies towards developing countries.
Charlotte, 18, Finland: I am active in a nationwide students' association which encourages youth to influence their environment. I have also been raising money for youth related development projects in the Third World.

Agata, 17, Poland: I have recently joined the Polish Ozone Group which writes essays and articles on all matters to do with ecology. We try to teach people and raise awareness. I shall work to spread the Rescue Mission in Poland.

Katya, 16, Russia: I work with Rzhev Peace Child group on plays and musicals on international themes. We really need the Rescue Mission in my country to make us feel united with the rest of the world.

Blanka, 17, Czech Republic: I'm a member of the Unesco Club in my town. We arrange exchanges with schools in other European countries. We have debates on education and development issues.

Daniela, 19, Croatia: I started Peace Child in Croatia doing international theatre programmes and leadership training in areas like Human Rights and Agenda 21. My major concern now is ending the war.

Ivan, 17, Serbia: With the war, it's impossible to do anything. We had a magazine by students, *What do you want?* It ran out of money and the editors went to the army. With the Rescue Mission, I hope we shall start a big youth campaign through all former Yugoslavia.

Chamsai, 17, Thailand: I work with the Greenspace Club which works to create environmental awareness throughout the school. I am hoping to set up a youth watchdog group to see that the government does Agenda 21.

Birce, 17, Turkiye: We don't have a club but kids in my school are very concerned about the environment. We plant trees and have talks about the air pollution problems in our city, which are sometimes bad enough to close the school.

Andreanna & Portia, 11, Philippines: We belong to Environmentalists in the Class-room. We ensure the whole school is clean - it's hard because students are so untidy. Many of us demonstrated for a total ban on logging in our country. It's horrible when you go out into the country: all the hills are bald. The Department of Environment & Natural resources ignored us. We need a Day of Access!

Anuragini, 20, India: I work with "Kalpavriksh" a student environment group fighting to preserve a 7,777 hectare Ridge which they are threatening to "develop" into a park. It is the last piece of unspoilt land in our city region. We also fight for a cleaner city.
Rekha, 14, India: To tell the truth, I haven't done anything until the Agenda 21 work. No child does, because children don't think they have any power. I am so amazed to see how much power we could have.

Suhail, 18, Tanzania: I helped found Roots and Shoots in Dar es Salaam two years ago and helped it spread nationally and internationally. It is run entirely by students. We do projects on protecting coral reefs, mangrove swamps and the Red Colobus Monkey which is unique to Zanzibar.

Jeremy, 15, Australia: I organised the Voice of the Children hearings in my state last year bringing the concerns of kids to state legislators. This year, we go nationwide. I also edited books of Children's concerns and ideas. We're publishing the third this year.

CHILDREN AT RIO

*Coming here today, I have no hidden agenda. I am fighting for my future...
At school, you teach us to behave in the world. You teach us not to fight with
others, to work things out, to respect others, to clean up our mess, not to hurt
other creatures, to share and not be greedy. Then why do you go out and do
those things you teach us not to do?*
Severn Cullis-Suzuki, 12, to the Rio Earth Summit, June 1992

RIO'S SHADOW

Youth had their own summit in Rio. In March 1992 young people aged between 15 and 30 converged on San Jose, Costa Rica to prepare for the Earth Summit. It was a unique gathering 300 young people from 97 countries, 75% from developing countries 50% female and 10% indigenous - an exact replica of the world's population. Out of the week emerged the Youth Statement to Rio, a powerful statement dealing with issues from poverty to pollution.

But the youth were not as lucky as Severn Suzuki. She tried to speak for children who had no voice at Rio and she was great: she got a standing ovation! But the voiceless children didn't ask her to speak: the director of UNICEF did. In truth, she represented herself.

YOUTH GAGGED

Official youth were promised an hour. Young people are half of the world's population, so one hour in 14 days seemed fair. When they arrived, they were told they only had ten minutes. Two minutes in, the TV cameras were turned off; reporters watching in the press room couldn't hear. When the youth tried to tell the eager press what they'd said, UN police arrested them for holding an "illegal press conference"! So what everyone remembers is images of kids being hauled off by police, nothing of the statement. It said things like all Third World debt should be cancelled because rich counties had earned more than enough out of the period of colonialism. A bit radical, but that's the way youth should be. No diplomatic games.

Children were also snubbed. A group called Voice of the Children had organized hearings around the world. It was the Prime Minister of Norway's idea and she promised to bring six world leaders to hear their statement. None came. She didn't even turn up herself. But a US Senator did come. He discussed the kids ideas in a great way. Two weeks later, he became Bill Clinton's running mate. He is now Vice President Al Gore!

Ivan Sekulovic, 17, Serbia

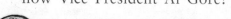

BLACK HOLES IN AGENDA 21

The Youth Statement was important because is pointed out many black holes in Agenda 21. Young people can - and must! - speak out on matters that governments cannot or dare not talk about. Black holes in Agenda 21 include:

WAR AND MILITARISM: Nothing destroys the environment and wrecks development quicker than war or the billions spent preparing for it. No mention in Agenda 21!

GOVERNANCE: The Agenda suggests no new government structures to implement even its own proposals let alone the ones it leaves out. We need a new way of governing the whole planet. The problems we face are bigger than any single country.

DISCRIMINATION and NATIONALISM: Nazism lives! Europe is witnessing a neo-Nazi resurrection. Nationalism is causing mayhem in ex-USSR and ex-Yugoslavia. Nothing on this in Agenda 21.

> **"** I think we need to stop speaking about fascists in hushed tones - we should laugh at them. I would paint that stadium in Berlin pink! That's what I would do.
> Bono Vox, U2 **"**

BIRTH CONTROL: Powerful lobbies mobilized opposition to this from many quarters. It was not seriously addressed in the Agenda, and not given any of the funding it needs.

RENEWABLE ENERGY SOURCES - solar, wind, wave power, etc. Oil-exporting countries insisted these be played down.

MULTINATIONALS: A planned chapter on control of multinationals was left out.

REFUGEES: Several of us witnessed the tragedy of refugees in our own countries. The Agenda says little to them.

NUCLEAR DISARMAMENT: The Cold War ended and just when we thought it was safe to fill in the shelters, we hear that 25 countries are keen to join the nuclear club!

HUMAN RIGHTS - are mentioned but is development a human right? This is a vital question to four fifths of the world who need development urgently. Nothing in Agenda 21.

CONSUMPTION: The chapter on consumption became weaker during the run-up to Rio. No firm directions on Green Taxes and environmental accounting were made.

MEDIA: The influence of TV, radio and the newspapers is immense. So is their responsibility. Countries have different views on how to deal with media but no attempt was made to reach a consensus on this in Rio.

From The Road to the 21st Century *Neil Steward, 17, UK*

RIGHT TO BE HEARD

Each country should include children's concerns in all relevant policies for environment and development and support their involvement in the United Nations.   Agenda 21, chapter 25

"You children of today are the hope for tomorrow" How many times have we heard that? It's true but are we to wait twiddling our thumbs till we become adults? No! Agenda 21 and the Convention on the Rights of the Child give us the right to be heard; with the environment collapsing and the population rising by 4-5 billion in our lifetimes, we must speak out for the future!

THE SOURCE OF POWER

Agenda 21 and the Convention ...
Within these documents, power lies waiting to be seized and used! The law on Child Rights, signed by 148 governments, gives children the right to participate in decisons that affect them. These decisions can range from issues such as, pollution at a local pond, to international problems of hazardous waste dumping. So speak up!! Excercise your right. Therein lies your power.

> **"** *I have absolutely no doubt that children are leaders where environmental matters are concerned. They have the power to educate their parents as decision-makers and change what's happening at an individual level.*
> **Elizabeth Dowdeswell, Executive Director, UNEP** **"**

Chamsai Menasveta, 17, Thailand

> **"** *The law on children's rights has three parts: provision, (of food, medical care, education, etc.); protection (from child labour, adult abuse, under the law etc.) and participation by children. Few governments have any philosophic problem with the first two. It's the third part that worries them.*
> **Richard Reid, Director, Public Affairs, UNICEF** **"**

DAY OF ACCESS

Each country should provide children the opportunity to present their views on government decisions.

Agenda 21, chapter 25

How do we pierce the deaf ears of politicians and be heard above their own talk? We need to give them a hearing aid: a Day of Access - one day every year when leaders and officials at all levels of government have to listen to our concerns.

WHAT *IS* THE IDEA....?

There are two main goals behind this idea:

1. To remind leaders of the long-term needs of children and get them to change their policies in line with what we'll need in the future;

2. To check up on how far we've got in implementing Agenda 21, Human Rights, and all the other promises they've made in the past.

In order for a Day of Access to work, we have to <u>be informed</u> about what's going on, what they've promised etc. Hopefully, this book will have given you some ideas of what you need to talk about.

Second, we have to be organize so that each year, kids follow up on what kids have asked before. We talk about that more on the next page, but first let's look at some countries where a Day of Access for Children already exists.

Voice of the Children

On October 27th 1992, 35 young people gathered in Parliament House, Sydney to declare their proposals on all the issues that affected them. Top Australian politicians, business leaders and the media were out in force to listen. It was perhaps the first time in Australia's history that young people were recognized as having something worthwhile to say.

How was it done? A committee of high profile people got behind it. A competition was widely advertized giving young people aged 12-18 the chance to come up with innovative proposals for new laws. The best were declared on Voice of the Children Day.

Making the proposals come true is the hard part. After loads of follow-up meetings with politicians and other leaders, the roposals on drunk driving and juvenile justice have been taken up; 13 year old Sue-Lyn Chan's Car-Free Day idea is hitting the streets.Best of all, in 1994, Voice of the Children Day will become a National Event! For young Australians, this is a good start.

Jeremy Heimans, 15, Australia

Turkey delights!

In Turkey, fiction has already become fact. Every year on April 23rd, Turkish youth get access to their leaders! In fact, the whole day is devoted to youth, from presentations at the local stadium, to youth centered TV programs. More importantly, youth get to speak to the decision-makers, from the Prime Minister, to the city Mayors, and if the ideas are valuable, they are adopted. I wish this could be an international meeting and all children, chosen by their friends as representatives of their countries could come to Turkey and bring their peace messages from their country. I wish that they had the right to access their leaders as we do, but in a more democratic fashion.

Birce Boga, 17, Turkiye (Turkey)

Chamsai Menasveta, 17, Thailand

GETTING IT TOGETHER

If I was a child today, I'd be worried. If you think you can solve the problems we face by recycling a few cans, you'll get to 2040 and find you've been duped. The world will be a mess because you won't have dealt with the main problem which is the widening gap between rich and poor. The great challenge of the 21st century is to reduce your consumption or face war between rich and poor.

Warren Lindner, Director, Center for Our Common Future

As we edited this book, we thought of the thousands of kids who have worked on it who'd like to be here with us now. We've read their summaries, seen their pictures and they've inspired us. We'd like kids everywhere to become a part of this Rescue Mission, to get access to leaders with their ideas and concerns. It cannot just be an elite. There's only one way to do this in a fair way: to build a Global Democracy of Children.

The journey of a thousand miles begins with just a single step. **Old Chinese Proverb**

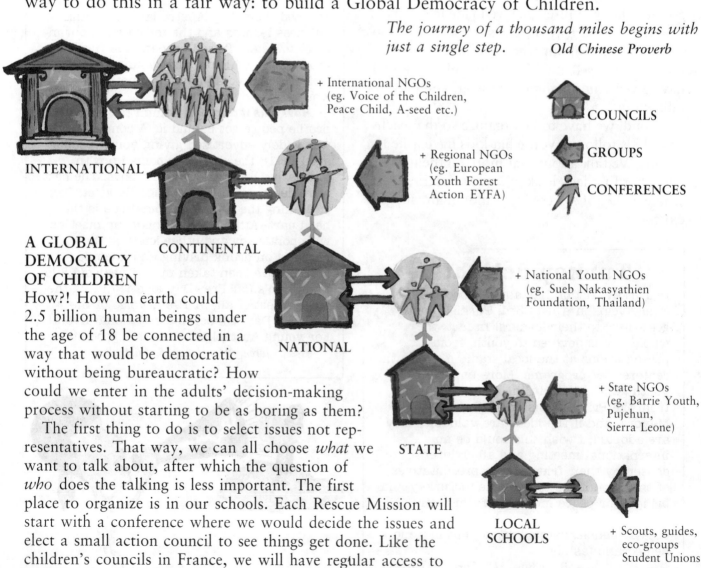

+ International NGOs (eg. Voice of the Children, Peace Child, A-seed etc.)

INTERNATIONAL

+ Regional NGOs (eg. European Youth Forest Action EYFA)

COUNCILS

GROUPS

CONFERENCES

CONTINENTAL

+ National Youth NGOs (eg. Sueb Nakasyathien Foundation, Thailand)

NATIONAL

+ State NGOs (eg. Barrie Youth, Pujehun, Sierra Leone)

STATE

LOCAL SCHOOLS

+ Scouts, guides, eco-groups Student Unions

YOU!

A GLOBAL DEMOCRACY OF CHILDREN

How?! How on earth could 2.5 billion human beings under the age of 18 be connected in a way that would be democratic without being bureaucratic? How could we enter in the adults' decision-making process without starting to be as boring as them?

The first thing to do is to select issues not representatives. That way, we can all choose *what* we want to talk about, after which the question of *who* does the talking is less important. The first place to organize is in our schools. Each Rescue Mission will start with a conference where we would decide the issues and elect a small action council to see things get done. Like the children's councils in France, we will have regular access to local government and work with them, perhaps to organize the Local Agenda 21.

With experience at the local level, we'll be ready to ask for access to state governments. Representatives from all local councils in our state, region or province will take priority issues decided by local conferences and discuss them at a state conference, again, electing a council to see that things get done. This council would work with state governments to make sure things get done.

The final goal is to move on to national, continental and international levels - a step-ladder the things that concern you and me can be carried to the highest levels of power. This is the kind of structure we need to make the Rescue Mission work.

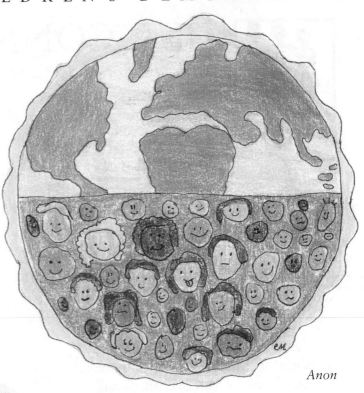

Anon

INFORMATION NETWORK

The key to it all is keeping in touch with each other. This is hard to do with the language differences, distances, phone bills etc. The solution is to set up a series of Youth Centres around the world, run by young people from different countries. Their job would be to help set up and promote the Action Councils and to keep in touch with each other. The Rescue Mission will be promoted chiefly through the many existing eco-groups, scouts, guides etc. The Youth Centres will simply promote and network their work and success around the world.

Children and governments in the rich world must help pay for centres to be set up in developing countries. Young people from rich and poor countries will work together to making each centre like a youth United Nations - a place where anybody can get the information they want on global problems. It would also be a place where local young people can meet, hang out and chat. Working there for 6 months to a year should be an option to replace National Service.

Al Gore sees the Rescue Mission as a way of collecting eco-information. Many of us do that already and it would be good to network that information globally. But this structure could do other things, especially help developing countries. If Mr Gore is serious about partnership, we hope that he will sit down and hear our ideas as well.

THE DAY OF ACCESS

That means access. Something we've never had. Sure we've had photo-opportunities: politicians standing surrounded by kids, or kissing babies. Now we need them really to listen to us. The day could be on different days in different countries but once a year, perhaps on the International Day of Peace (3rd Tuesday in September), we would gather all the results and tell the general public what our leader's have said - how far they kept the promises they made to us the previous year.

Who can participate? Anyone under the age of 18. Non-voters. Older people will be welcome as staff and advisers; (*remember - Agenda 21 is about making partnerships!*) But under 18s will be in control.

THE BILL?

The cost of putting together youth-run local offices throughout the world with phones, fax machines etc. we calculate would come to about US$258 million. A lot of money but small change compared to Agenda 21's total bill of $600 billion.

TARGET DATES

1995 - Pilot local offices in every region
1998 - National meetings in every country
2000 - Complete global democracy of youth

GET CONNECTED

Anybody, Somebody and Everybody knew there was a job to be done. Anybody could do it and Everybody thought that Somebody would do it. But in the end, Nobody did it.

We must understand that the only ones who can make the Day of Access happen is us! No one really wants to listen to us. They will come and listen nicely to us, be photographed, pat us kindly on the head and send us on our way. To bring it to life it needs our energy, our effort.

We've found that being together working on this book makes us feel incredibly powerful. We all dread going home - being alone again. That's why we are determined to stay in touch with the way we feel now. Just knowing that there are people like us, concerned about the same things on the other side of the world, helps. If you feel the same, get connected! Together, we will be unstoppable.

Viola, 12, Italy

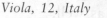

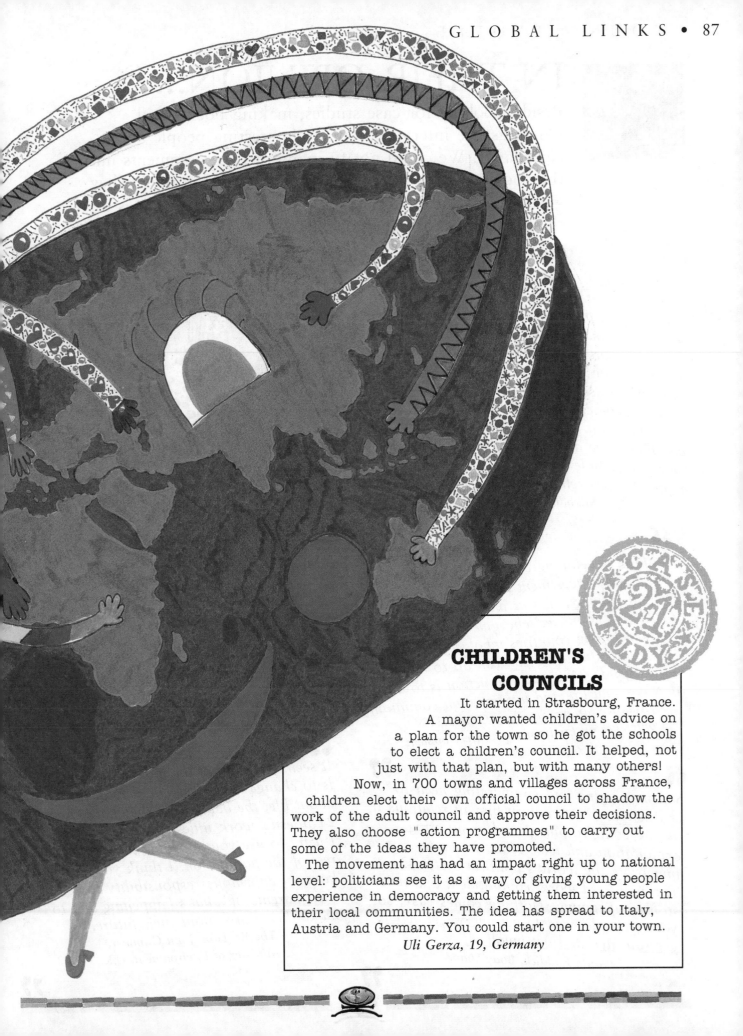

CHILDREN'S COUNCILS

It started in Strasbourg, France. A mayor wanted children's advice on a plan for the town so he got the schools to elect a children's council. It helped, not just with that plan, but with many others!

Now, in 700 towns and villages across France, children elect their own official council to shadow the work of the adult council and approve their decisions. They also choose "action programmes" to carry out some of the ideas they have promoted.

The movement has had an impact right up to national level: politicians see it as a way of giving young people experience in democracy and getting them interested in their local communities. The idea has spread to Italy, Austria and Germany. You could start one in your town.

Uli Gerza, 19, Germany

IN THEIR OPINION...

Besides looking for case studies, making poems and paintings, we interviewed many interesting people about Agenda 21. We could not fit many of their comments into the book but they were in our minds as we worked. They gave us a background and sense of how important it is to think hard now about the next century.

> *The preceding generations have done much that is good but also much that will have to be undone - both within each country and in the international community. Like you, I feel that politicians and governments are too slow in taking urgently-needed decisions. But I urge you to seek to effect change only through democratic means. Never resort to force. The 20th century has demonstrated too well that force does not solve problems. You have your whole lives ahead of you - make it happy for yourselves and for others.*
>
> Mikhail Gorbachev

> *Helping developing countries is not foreign aid. It's an investment in global environmental security. It is as important for the developed countries who give aid as it is for the developing countries who receive it. The most powerful thing you can do to make sure Agenda 21 is put into action is to do it in your own life and in your own community.*
>
> Maurice Strong, Secretary General, UN
> Conference on Environment & Development

> *Sharing, caring and co-operating need to characterize 21st century human relations if we are going to put an end to suffering, exploitation and war. How do we re-invigorate the world's political systems? Through hard work, commitment and non-stop campaigning. Nothing comes easy, so young people need to get angry, get active, get educated and get involved.*
>
> Anita Roddick, Body Shop

> *It seems to me that the most important thing is to change attitudes. The way people think about life, the habits that they have. Agenda 21 doesn't work unless people make it work. I want to use young people to sensitise all the rest of the population. I think young people have an enormous responsibility to remind their parents of what's happening and to make them care about their future.*
>
> The Rt. Hon. John Gummer,
> Minister of Environment, U.K.

"The real importance of Agenda 21 is that it "responsibilitizes" all of us. No one sector of society is going to make it happen, no one country, no one United Nations. It's all of us.

Tariq Banuri,
Sustainable Development Institute of Pakistan"

Viola, 12, Italy

"We asked this wise, wise man many questions - 'Who's going to do this? How do we force this governments or that company to act?'... Always he steered our thoughts away from thinking what other people might or might not do, to what we could do ourselves. That's where Agenda 21 really begins: with us!

Report on an interview with
Tommy Koh, Singapore"

"For me the most important challenges are the alleviation of poverty, changing consumption patterns and reducing population growth. If we want to say that the world has become more sustainable, we have to see significant progress on these three areas. Also, people need to accept the responsibility to others and to future generations. The message of Agenda 21 is to encourage as many people as possible to connect with each other - to exchange experiences and to seek answers.

Nitin Desai, Under-Secretary-General,
Policy Coordination & Sustainable Development"

"At the end of every discussion, we always come back to the question of consumption. You can't bring up a new generation of people telling them they can have everything we have and more. They can have more but we will have to measure its quality differently and measure poverty differently as well. We're living on a borrowed planet here. It's critical that young people grow up with a concept of their place in the community and their place on the planet which is different from the one made by the last two generations. They have to see themselves in the context of the whole ecosystem.

Rachel Kyte, Director,
Women for Environment and Development"

"We must reconcile the relationship between humans and nature. Find the balance and respect it. I just hope that the energy you have now writing this book doesn't dissipate by the time you grow up and move into the positions where you can do something. What's important is to maintain the energy needed for change. Having more women in charge would be a good place to start.

Kevin Godley, MediaLab, One World"

Jalal Eddine Kokodin, 17, Morocco

WAVES OF PEACE

Carefully listen as dusk arrives
to the quiet song of the sea
Listen to the waves as they whisper
They have something to say to thee -

"Children walk ahead where your parents
          don't dare
 born to be arrows of peace
 To dance where all hope's buried
 to bring light where there's sorrow and
          disease

 You have got the key to tomorrow
 You are the ones who still can feel
 Use this power with wisdom
 use this power to heal

Join your hands and you'll be strong
Like a restless river you'll flow
Just like us, the waves, you'll sweep the shore
And the truth in your voice will glow

Don't be afraid, don't lose your faith
whereever your heart leads you
There are no walls, no limits remain
when you believe in what you do
          Mia Björkqvist, 19, Finland

CHARLIE

Hello! My name is Charlie and I'm six years old. I
have one brother and one sister. We live in a nice
house next to a clean river. Everyone in our
neighbourhood is happy. Until the "plant" arrived.
It was to give jobs and make us all happy, but the
air started to smoke. It was hard to breathe deep.
Our nice river was turning brown. We all ignored it
for we had hope.
We waited ...
People started getting sick and my mother was ill
very often. She coughed a lot, but we had hope!
We waited ...
My mother was taken to a hospital. She had lung
cancer. People were leaving our nice
neighbourhood.
We still had hope!   We waited ...
My little sister got lead poisoned but not severely.
Now we drunk bottled water.
We had hope. We waited ...
I don't want to wait anymore. Something has to be
done. I don't want anyone to be hurt any more.
I have hope.   **Jon Hafmer, Thailand**

Diana Lucia Rey Sanchez, 11, Colombia

Michael Kanyako, 22, Sierra Leone

So you've reached the end of this book. But this is not the end of the story! Every one can take action for a better world.

Often we feel powerless. We think we cannot change anything until we grow up. Well, remember Samantha Smith: she helped end the Cold War with her letter to Andropov when she was only 10. Joan of Arc drove the English out of France before she was 19; Mozart wrote half of his music before he was 21!

But this is not only about child prodigies. The daily efforts of each one of us are at least as important. What matters is the voice of your heart. Let it be heard!

- if you are a painter, paint with great passion;
- if you are a writer, write with great passion;
- if you are an environmentalist, defend nature with all your heart.

This is your invitation to help. Your Rescue Mission is about to begin!

GLOSSARY

Acid rain Rain with acid in it.

Atmosphere The envelope of air which surrounds our Earth.

Biodiversity A word to describe all the plants and animals that exist in nature.

Biosphere The living air and/or water in which animals live.

Biotechnology The technology of life: explores ways by which life forms are engineered.

Boycott Avoid.

Capacity Ability.

Capacity-building Creating the ability in people and nations to do things.

CFCs Short for Chloro-fluorocarbons, chemicals which attack and destroy the ozone layer.

Child In the past, referred to people under 15; under the new Child Rights law, it refers to people under 18.

Chronic Going on for a long time as in Chronic Disease.

Compost Rotted vegetables or sewage that you put on your garden to fertilize it.

Condemn To blame or bring judgement upon.

Consciousness Awakeness. Also means knowing what you're talking about.

Consequences Results.

Consumption The act of consuming or eating.

Contaminated Poisoned or dirtied.

Contraception Birth control.

Conversion The act of changing something into something else.

Coordinate Bring together.

Deforestation Clearing land of trees.

Degrade To make worse *(noun = degradation)*

Democracy Rule by all the people.

Deplete To use up *(noun = depletion)*

Desalination The way fresh water is made out of sea water.

Desertification Process by which land becomes degraded.

Diarrhoea Runny tummy; disease of bowel.

Drought Long period without rain.

Disempowered Made powerless.

Ecosystem Who eats who or what. Food chain that links animals and plants in the same area.

Empower Giving some one, eg. a child, power and confidence to do things.

Environment All the things around us - plants and animals, air and water, and land.

Erosion Wearing away of land or rock by wind and water.

Exploit Take advantage of.

Fertile Productive; able to grow crops.

Fertilize Make fertile *(noun=fertilizer)*

Finite Something with an end *(Infinite=something without end)*

Global warming General description of the problem of pollution in the atmosphere which causes the Earth's surface to warm up.

Greenhouse effect The effect that causes global warming; the atmosphere becomes like a greenhouse.

Guinea-worm disease Horrible disease caused by invisible worm that enters the body from water.

Habitat Where a particular group of plants or animals live.

Hazards Dangers.

Hazardous waste Dangerous garbage/rubbish.

Hectare A measure of area *(2 acres approx.)*

Illiterate Not able to read *(noun=illiteracy)*

Implement To get done *(noun=implementation)*

Indigenous Native = people who have lived in the same place for hundreds or thousands of years, like the Aborigines of Australia.

Integrate To bring together; eg. things or ideas.

Leprosy Horrible disease which slowly eats away your body *(people with leprosy = lepers)*

Liana A climbing plant of tropical forest.

Malaria Feverous disease which attacks you in the tropics. Caught from mosquito bites.

Massacre Murdering hundreds/thousands of people (or trees!) at a time.

Measles Common disease that thousands of children die from it in poor countries.

Minimize Make as small as possible.

Mortal Something that dies *(noun=mortality)*

Mutated Changed.

Multinational Large corporation or company with offices and/or factories in several nations.

Oppressive Being oppressed = made to do things you don't want to do.

Ozone layer The protective layer of ozone gas which blocks out the Sun's harmful ultraviolet rays.

Pesticide Chemical which kills bugs and pests.

Polio Disease almost wiped out but still causes many children to die in poor countries.

Pollution The dirtying of the air, land or water.

Population programme Programmes to inform parents how to manage the size of their families.

Post-Colonial After the period of colonization (ownership) of poor countries by the rich.

Priority Most important thing.

Process Way by which things get done.

Protectionism Customs taxes that protect national industries by making foreign goods more expensive.

Rain forest Jungle. Tropical forests where there is heavy rainfall.

Recycling The act of reusing something to make something else; not throwing things away.

Refugee Someone forced to leave their home by war or natural disaster, like an earthquake.

Rehabilitate Make good again; make something work again.

Renewable Something that can be renewed - used over and over again without running out like solar energy.

River blindness Horrible sickness which makes people blind; caught from dirty rivers.

Sanitation System to get rid of sewage and waste water.

Strategies Plans.

Susceptible Easily persuaded by arguments.

Sustainable development Meeting the needs of the present generation without harming the ability of future generations to meet their needs.

Technology The science of engineering.
Third World Poor countries. Also known as the developing world or the "South" as in North=rich and South=poor.
Toxic waste Poisonous garbage/rubbish.
Tuberculosis Disease which causes your lungs to rot which prevents you breathing.
Ultraviolet radiation Sun's rays that give you a great tan and skin cancer.
Unsustainable A process or life-style that cannot be kept up indefinitely.
UN United Nations.

UNDP UN Development Programme.
UNEP UN Environment Programme.
UNESCO UN Educational, Scientific and Cultural Organization.
UNICEF UN Children's Fund
Vaccines Medicine which doctors inject into you to prevent you getting bad diseases.
Vulnerable Weak; capable of being exploited.
Young people Children and youth in new and old definitions.
Youth Used to be 15-25 year olds; now applied to people 18-30.

INDEX

AGENDA 21 TASK FORCE

This book is a result of thousands of hours of work by over 10,000 children in 200 groups in 75 countries around the world. They are the members of the Children's Agenda 21 task force. We invite you to join them:

ALBANIA
Children's Cultural Centre, Lidiana Morcka
ARGENTINA
FUNDECMA, Cordoba
FUNAM/Voice of the Children, Cordoba
Guia-Scouts, Roca
AUSTRALIA
St Kilian's Primary School, Bendigo
A.M.E. School, Canberra,
Voice of the Children, Sydney
AUSTRIA
Intercultural Learning Club, Vienna
BANGLADESH
Brain-work of Budlet Community
BARBADOS
Barbados Environmental Youth Programme
BELARUS
UNESCO Club, Minsk
Peace Child Friendship Club, Gomel
BELGIUM
Koninklijk Athenacum, Gent
St John's Eco Club, Waterloo
BOLIVIA
Ninos del Serpaj, La Paz
BRAZIL
American School of Rio de Janeiro
BULGARIA
Bistra Rubinova, Sofia
Unesco Club of Varna
BURKINO FASO
Lycée Zinda & Collége Notre Dame,
Ouagadougou
CANADA
Spruce Glen School, Huntsville, Ontario
Woodstock High School, New Brunswick
CHAD
Cours de Soir, Club UNESCO Belle-vue
CHILE
Chilean Agenda 21 Task Force, Santiago
CHINA
Beijing Jingshan School
COLOMBIA
Inem Santiago Perez El Tunal, Sur
COSTA RICA
D.O.E., Country Day School, San José
Andrea Balestero, San Pedro
CROATIA
Peace Child Croatia, Zagreb
CYPRUS
Service Club, Falcon School, Nicosia
CZECH REPUBLIC
Basic School, Homi Marsov
Zdklani skola, Hradec Králové
UNESCO Club, Olomouc
ZO CSOP Gymnasium, Strakonicc
Iva Opletalova, IDM MSMT, Prague
Gymnasium T.G.M., Litvinov
DJIBOUTI
A. Idris, UNICEF
ECUADOR
Asociacion Scouts del Ecuador, Quito
ESTONIA
Children & Youth Theatre, Tallinn
ETHIOPIA
Menelik II Comp-Sec Nature Club, Addis
Ababa
EGYPT
American International School in Egypt

FINLAND
Mattlidens Gymnasium, Esbo
Puolalanmäki School, Turku
FRANCE
Lycée Helene Boucher, Paris
College Musselburgh, Champigny
GEORGIA
Youth Eco-Movement, Tbilisi
GERMANY
Benediktiner Gymnasium, Ehal
GRENADA
St Josephs Convent, St George's
GUATAMALA
Voices of the Children National Campaign
HAITI
Monique Clesca, UNICEF
HUNGARY
Training College, Nyiregyhaza
INDIA
Vidyodaya School, Madras
DB Gayathri, Mysore, Karnatka
Sadaak Chaap (Federation of Street Children)
Bombay
Manava Bharati International School,
New Delhi
India UNESCO Clubs, (INFUCA), Mangalore
Tamilnadu UNA, Madras
Kalpavriksh Environment Action Group,
New Delhi
Alpha Movement, Calcutta
WWF India, New Delhi
World Children's Centre, Hyderabad
Mainak & Friends, Durgapur, W. Bengal
Fr. Agnel School, New Delhi
Children & Trees Project, Auroville
Young Naturalists NCI, Jamnagar
St James School, Calcutta
INDONESIA
IKIP, Jakarta
IRELAND
Environmental Conservation Org. for Youth
(ECO)
ITALY
Brigitte Beretta, Milano
Istituto Magistrale Margherita di Savoia,
Napoli
United World College of the Adriatic
JAPAN
Peace Child Hiroshima
JORDAN
Amman Baccalaureate School
Help Environment Love Peace (HELP)
Amman New Camp, Unesco School
KENYA
Lenana School, Nairobi
Tom Mboya School, Mbita
Loreto Convent Msongari
KOSOVO
Peace Child Pristina
MADAGASCAR
Club Unesco, Antanarivo
MALAWI
MALAYSIA
Penang Free School
MALTA
ECO Club, Valletta
UNESCO Club, Hamrun
Lily of the Valley School, Mosta

MAURITANIA
Terre Vivante, Nouakchott
MEXICO
Colegio Bilbao, Cuajimalpa
Aaron Hawkins, Oaxaca
NEW ZEALAND
Peace Through Unity Youth Forum
Rainbow Theatre, Wanganui
NIGERIA
Peace Child Nigeria, Ada Amoji
Immaculate Conception School, Uyo
PANAMA
Colegio Javier, Panama City
PHILIPPINES
Institute of Alternative Futures
Green Forum, Metro Manila
Miriam College
Children & Peace, JASMS, Quezon City
POLAND
Polish Ozone Group, Krakow
I Liceum Ogolnoksztalcace, Krakow
Artur Marsy, Wroclaw
Class of Cultural Heritage, Warsaw
ZHP Byczyna, Mandriga Myroslaw
UNOY-Net Katowice
Children's Parliament of Silesia, Chorzow
"Inkubator", Warsaw
PORTUGAL
British School, Oporto
RWANDA-ZAIRE
UNESCO Club, Cyangugu
RUSSIA
Club Baltic Seagull, School 61,
St Petersburg
School No 3, Ulan Udé, Mongolia
Peace Child Krasnoyarsk
Peace Child Theatre Group, Rzhev, Tver
SIERRA LEONE
Port Loko UN Students Association
(PLUNSA)
Fourah Bay College, Freetown
SINGAPORE
Baha'i Youth Committee
SLOVAKIA
Pali Safárik University, Presov
SOUTH AFRICA
Disabled Peoples International, Natal
Deborah Sack, Capetown
SPAIN
Seminario Ciencas Naturas, Santiago
SRI LANKA
Environmental Society, Colombo
International School
Kokila (Cuckoo) Club, Imbilgoda
SUDAN
International School of Khartoum
SWEDEN
Björn Carlson, Sigtuna School
SWITZERLAND
International School of Geneva
TAIWAN
Global Awareness & Action Club,
US School, Taipei
TANZANIA
Roots & Shoots, Zanzibar
International School of Tanganyika
Amani Unesco Club, Miwara
Azania Secondary School Fine Art Club

AGENDA 21

Throughout the book, we include quotes of the original Agenda 21 to give you a taste of it. Here is the full list of chapter titles:

1. Preamble

Section One: Social and Economic Dimensions
2. International Cooperation in Trade
3. Combating Poverty
4. Changing Consumption Patterns
5. Population and Sustainability
6. Protecting Human Health
7. Sustainable Human Settlements
8. Integrating Decision-making

Section Two: Conservation and Management of Natural Resources
9. Protecting the Atmosphere
10. Sustainable Land Management
11. Combating Deforestation
12. Combating Desertification and Drought
13. Sustainable Mountain Development
14. Sustainable Agriculture and Rural Development
15. Conservation of Biological Diversity
16. Management of Biotechnology
17. Protecting and Managing the Oceans
18. Protecting and Managing Fresh Water
19. Safe Use of Toxic Chemicals
20. Management of Hazardous Wastes
21. Management of Solid Waste and Sewage
22. Managing Radioactive Waste

Section Three: Strengthening the Role of Major Groups
23. Preamble
24. Women in Sustainable Development
25. Children and Youth in Sustainable Development
26. Strengthening the Role of Indigenous People
27. Partnerships with NGOs
28. The Role of Local Authorities
29. The Role of Workers and Trade Unions
30. Business and Industry
31. The Role of Science and Technology
32. The Role of Farmers

Section Four: Means of Implementation
33. Financing Sustainable Development
34. Technology Transfer
35. Science for Sustainable Development
36. Education, Training and Public Awareness
37. Capacity Building for Sustainable Development
38. International Institutions for Sustainable Development
39. Revision of International Laws
40. Information for Decision-making

If you're interested, the complete text is now available in all six UN Languages (English, French, Spanish, Russian, Chinese and Arabic) from UN Information Centres (UNICs) in most capital cities. Agenda 21 and many other Rio documents are available from the Centre for Our Common Future; these include a plain language edition of Agenda 21: *Agenda for Change* which has been invaluable to us: 70-pages long with 2-3 page summaries of each chapter plus charts and diagrams, it is a useful next step. The Centre also produces news-letters on what governments and the UN are doing to follow-up on Agenda 21. Peace Child International is one of the Centre's working partners. Contact them direct at: **Centre for Our Common Future**, 52 rue de Paquis, 1201 GENEVA, Switzerland

THAILAND
Greenspace Club, Intl. School, Bangkok
TRINIDAD
Sixth Form Secondary, St James
St Stephen's College, Princes Town
Tranquillity Government School, Port of Spain
Naparima Girls High School, San Fernando
TUNISIA
UNICEF, Juliette Sayegh
TURKEY
Anadolu High School, Bursa
Eyyup Sabri Guler, Ankara
UNITED KINGDOM
The Norton School, Stockton on Tees
Onslow St. Audreys, Hatfield
St Christophers, Letchworth
St Mary's Convent, Bishop's Stortford
Stowmarket Middle School, Suffolk
United World College, Wales
Bridgeforth College, Derry, Northern Ireland
Connor Channing, Derry, Northern Ireland
UNITED STATES
Andrew College, Cuthbert, Georgia
CAPE, Ingrid Kavanagh, Austin, Texas

Creative Response, York, Pennsylvania
Cuauhtemoc Art Center, Berkeley, California
E Magazine, Connecticut
Kids FACE, Nashville, Tennessee
The Kinkaid School, Houston, Texas
Laurel Springs Env. Project, California
Milton Academy, Massachusetts (LORAX)
Parish Resource Centre, Mishawaka, Indiana
Peace Child Repertory Company, LA
Peace Child, Santa Cruz, California
Peace Child of the Low Country, Charleston
PS 99 Queens, New York
Results, Chevy Chase, Maryland
Seattle Peace Theatre, Washington State
Travis High School, Austin, Texas
Wilson Middle School, Carlisle, Pennsylvania
World Community Foundation, Albany, Georgia
URUGUAY
Grupo Ecologico Naturalera, Rio Negro
International School, Montivideo
YUGOSLAVIA
Children's Soros Project, Belgrade
Peace Child Belgrade

ZAMBIA
Trades UNESCO Club, Livingstone
Chongololu + Conservation Clubs, Lusaka
Life-Link Centre, Ndola
Many other people in many other countries contributed paintings collected for exhibitions arranged at the UN by the **UN Population Fund** and the **Save the Sea Campaign** of Japan. A big Thank You for the use of them. Also thanks to the wonderful *In Context* magazine, an excellent source of case studies and ideas. We'd also like to thank the following for their additional sponsorship: **Canon UK** for the photocopier; **L.A.W.N.** and **St Albans Sand & Gravel** for their sponsorship of our Indian and Nigerian editors; **Cameron Mackintosh** and **Principle Management** for their gifts of entertainment; **Herts County Council** for the use of the Hudnall Field Centre for the Editorial Meeting. Lastly, thanks to **Mark and Sue Stephens** for the gift of the office for this project, and to **Dr Noel Brown** of the UN Environment Programme who gave us the idea to make a Children's Edition.

Photograph Credits
p37 Tony Larkin; p32 UNICEF; p35 UNICEF; p36 UNICEF/Jeremy Horner *(top)* p40 UNHCR/A. Hollman *(top left)*; UNICEF Liaison/R.Nickelsberg *(top right)* p40/41 UNICEF/Jeremy Horner *(bottom)*; p42/43 UNICEF/Roger Lemoyne; p43 UNICEF/Jørgen Schytte *(top)*; p60 Chris Priestley; p66 Liaison/Robin Mayer; p68 Mark Edwards/Still Pictures *(right)*; p69 Herts County Council; p74 Caroline Penn/OXFAM;

We have made every effort to credit the contributors correctly. If there are any omissions or errors, please tell us and we will be happy to correct them in the reprints.

OVER TO YOU *Write to the Rescue Mission*

Rescue Mission Headquarters
Peace Child International Centre
The White House
Buntingford England SG9 9AH

Rescue Mission USA
11426-28 Rockville Pike
Suite 100
Rockville MD 20852 USA

At this point, books like this usually give you a list of addresses and "50 things you can do to save the environment." Given that things we need to do are changing all the time and are different depending on where you live, we are planning the *Rescue Mission Action Update*. Each issue will be written and designed by young people and include news on what's happening with Rescue Mission around the world, plus an exciting Action Challenge.

When you write, be sure to include your name and address. You'll receive free the latest Action Update and membership form. As a member, you'll become a correspondent and able to apply to come to work as an intern at Rescue Mission Headquarters. It is staffed by young people from all over the world – like a Youth United Nations!

JOIN US – WRITE TODAY!

WHAT IS PEACE CHILD?

In Papua New Guinea, when warring tribes of head-hunters made peace, each gave to the other a baby. The child grew up with the other tribe and if, in the future, conflict threatened, the tribes would send these children to resolve it. Such a child was called a Peace Child.

Peace Child International is a non-profit educational charity registered in England, the USA, The Netherlands, Russia and Israel with affiliated organizations in 30 other countries. Formed in 1981, it aims to give children the confidence they need to deal with the challenges they face in their lifetimes. The many programmes it produces include summer youth exchanges, book and play production. Its plays, *Peace Child* and *Earth Child*, have been performed more than 2,500 times in over 30 countries.

Rescue Mission is Peace Child's flagship project for the 1990s.

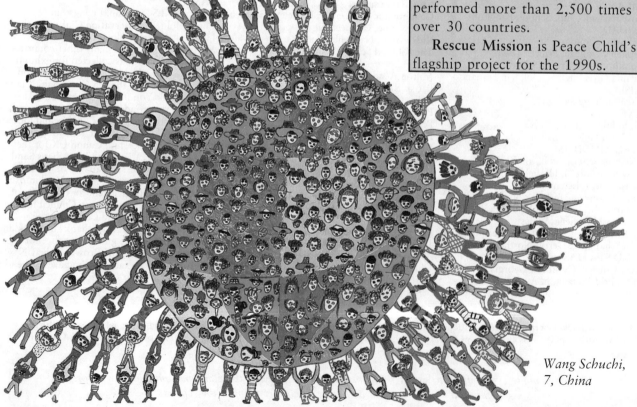

*Wang Schuchi,
7, China*

RESCUE MISSION:
Planet Earth

Children's
Activity
Booklet

by chiLDReN of the WoRLD
with an introduction by
Boutros Boutros-Ghali
Secretary-General
United Nations

RESCUE
MISSION
PLANET EARTH
A chiLDReN's edition of AGeNda 21

**PROJECT
LEARNING
TREE** Produced in cooperation with
Project Learning Tree®

Turning Agenda 21 into action is a big challenge for us all. Thousands of people at the United Nations and in governments are working on it. This booklet will show parents and educators how children can start to be a part of this work.

In three sections of the booklet, there are over a dozen activities that deal with air, water and land pollution. Children's views on these important issues are presented throughout *Rescue Mission*, most specifically on pages 10-13, 26-27 and 48-51.

Each section provides an overview of the problems and gives the children hands-on experience in finding solutions in ways they will understand and from which they will get satisfaction.

For example, children will have fun making action plans for conserving water in their own homes. The booklet will give them lots of ideas how to do this. It will show them how to discover air pollution and what to do about it.

Whether they do simple math calculations about gasoline pollution or observe wildlife in their backyard, using this booklet will help make your child a more eco-friendly citizen for the 21st Century.

These are familiar topics for children. They know about them from TV and news. We hope they will want to move on from these simple activities to the more complex challenges covered by the Rescue Mission Action Plan.

The views expressed in this booklet are those of its authors and do not reflect those of the book's sponsoring organizations.

AIR TO DRIVE
For ages 9 to 13

Materials needed:

Part A: a pair of athletic socks (or a white cloth rag); popsicle sticks, plastic wrap, two thermometers, and a tray of sprouted alfalfa, radish, or bean seeds in soil.

Part B: paper, pencil or pen, calculator (*optional*)

Overview

In these activities, children will become more aware of the relationship between cars, the earth's atmosphere and trees. They will explore the steps they can take to reduce automobile pollution and save energy.

Background

One of the reasons that life exists on earth is that the atmosphere acts like a greenhouse, allowing sunlight to enter while preventing heat from escaping. The earth's "greenhouse" is made up of gases in the atmosphere. Without these gases like carbon dioxide and water vapor the temperature of the earth would average -4 degrees instead of 60 degrees. But sometimes you can have too much of a good thing.

The burning of fossil fuels (coal, oil, gasoline, natural gas) produces large amounts of carbon dioxide and the percentage of this gas in the atmosphere is rising rapidly. As carbon dioxide levels increase so does the tendency of the atmosphere to trap heat. The overall effect could be a gradual warming of the earth, often referred to as "global climate change." This could lead to global changes such as rising ocean levels caused by melting of polar ice caps, flooding of coastal areas, changes in climate, extremes in weather patterns, and increased violence in weather such as hurricanes and tornadoes.

While the threat of global warming is under debate, most scientists agree on three things:

1) that there is a change in the percentage of gases in the atmosphere; **2)** that due to some of these changes we can probably expect an overall global change in temperature; and **3)** that such a change can have environmental consequences.

Plants offer a natural way to reduce the level of carbon dioxide in the atmosphere. Through the process called "photosynthesis," plants take huge amounts of carbon dioxide out of the atmosphere. An average young tree can remove about 25 pounds of carbon dioxide a year from the atmosphere. But that is only a little more than what is produced when one gallon of gasoline is burned.

Everybody has a role in reducing air pollution from automobiles — manufacturers who design more fuel efficient cars and families who find ways to reduce the amount they drive.

Part A: Tracking Down Invisible Pollution

Children may have trouble visualizing what's coming out of the tail pipe of a car since a lot of pollutants are hard to see (unless you're in a city like Los Angeles on a smoggy day!). Try the following demonstrations to illustrate how cars pollute and how the "greenhouse effect" works.

Demonstration 1: *Put a Sock on It (With adult participation only!)*

Here is an experiment that will dramatize the effect of car exhaust on air quality. (Before proceeding with the demonstration, make sure the car's exhaust pipe is cool to the touch and that the transmission is in "PARK" or "NEUTRAL, and that the car is on level ground with the emergency brake on.)

1 Take one white sock and place it tightly over the mouth of the car's tail pipe. Then the adult should start the car's engine (make sure the car is in the open air, rather than in a garage or closed space and children are well clear of the vehicle) and let it run for a few minutes.

2 Then, stop the engine and let the car cool down.

3 When the exhaust pipe is cool to the touch, take the sock off and compare it to the other sock. Chances are you will see large pollutant particles (ash, smoke, soot, etc.) from the exhaust trapped in the fabric, making it black. While smaller pollutant particles like ozone and carbon dioxide pass through the fabric, some larger ones do not. *(Note: A white rag torn in half can be used instead of socks. Secure one half of the rag over the exhaust pipe with a piece of fabric and proceed.)*

Demonstration 2: *Build a Greenhouse*

This experiment will show how the greenhouse effect can change the earth's temperature and also how plants help create moisture in the atmosphere.

1 Place a tent of plastic wrap over the seedling tray, using popsicle sticks or straws to create the tent.

2 Place one thermometer inside the tray and one outside the greenhouse.

3 Place the greenhouse near a window but not in direct sunlight.

4 After several hours, compare the temperatures both inside and outside the greenhouse. Also notice if there is water vapor trapped inside.

5 Which location is hotter and why? Which is wetter and why? Talk about how this shows the benefits of protective gases in the atmosphere (represented by the plastic wrap) and how plants help moisturize the environment.

Part B: Counting Carbon

1 Have the children keep track of the miles driven in the family car for a week. They can do this by noting the number on the odometer at the beginning and at the end of the week.

2 If one gallon of gas creates 20 pounds of carbon dioxide, have the children compute how much carbon dioxide has been created by the family car in that week. This can be done by dividing the number of miles by the miles per gallon of the average car (30 miles per gallon) and multiplying that by 20 pounds of carbon dioxide.
(*Example:* The car was driven 210 miles in a week. Divide that by 30 miles per gallon and the car will have used 7 gallons of gas. If each gallon creates 20 pounds of carbon dioxide, 7 gallons will create 140 pounds of carbon dioxide. So the family car can create 140 pounds of carbon dioxide in a week and 7,280 pounds in a year.)

3 If a tree can remove 25 pounds of carbon dioxide in a year, how many trees must be used to remove the carbon dioxide that the family car uses in a year?

Taking Action

1 Have the children plan a strategy for reducing the family's gasoline use. They could suggest more use of public transportation, car-pooling, combining errands, walking or bicycling, or other ideas. Have them calculate how many gallons of gas would be saved and how much less carbon dioxide would be produced. Try this strategy for a week.

2 Plant some trees. Every new tree planted will help save the atmosphere from pollution and global warming. A young tree can absorb 25 pounds of carbon dioxide from the atmosphere in a year.

EVERY DROP COUNTS!
For ages 9 to 13

Materials needed:

Part A: empty beverage container (1/2 gallon or 2-liter size), large measuring cup, watch with a second hand, paper, pencil or pen, calculator (optional)

Overview

It's easy to waste water, and even easier to take it for granted. It comes pouring out of our faucets as though it's in endless supply. But the truth is that fresh water supplies are dwindling. Fortunately it's just as easy to conserve water as it is to waste it. In these activities children will learn more about their family's water use and what they can do to diminish water waste.

Background

It's amazing how much water each of us uses every day. A seven-minute shower uses about 35 gallons of water. An average of six gallons goes down the drain with each flush of the toilet. Washing a load of laundry requires at least 35 gallons of water, and the list goes on. Individual Americans consume about 36 billion gallons of water a day. Add to that the water used by utilities, industry and agriculture, and the United States consumes 384 billion gallons a day. That's about 1,500 gallons for each person every day, which is the highest per capita use in the world. Canadians come in second at about 1,200 gallons per person a day.

Much of what we use daily is *groundwater*, which is water that fills the spaces between rocks and soil particles underground. The biggest source of groundwater is precipitation that has trickled down into the soil, such as rain or melting snow. This "trickle-down" process takes time; deep groundwater may require hundreds of years to replenish itself.

In many areas the rate at which groundwater replenishes itself cannot keep pace with the rate at which it is being used.

Whether our water supplies come from groundwater (as does half of the drinking water in the United States) or from lakes, streams, reservoirs, or other *surface water* sources, using too much water too fast can cause problems for people and wildlife.

If everyone made an effort to conserve water by making a few changes in their daily routines, huge amounts of water could be saved.

Part A: Water Watch

The best way to show children how much water the family uses is to let them observe and calculate the information themselves. These activities and accompanying charts will give them a much better understanding.

Demonstration 1: *Water Detectives*

1 Give the children the empty beverage container and tell them how much water it holds. Have them predict how much water they use in a day. Do they think it is more or less than the amount in the container? If so, how much more or less? Have them write their estimates down.

2 Now have them monitor their water use at home for a day. To do this, they will have to record every time they use water and the amount of water they use. (The chart that follows will help them determine the amount of water each activity consumes.)

3 After determining how much water they use in one day, have them monitor their water use while using various conservation suggestions like: taking shorter showers, turning off the water while brushing their teeth, and making sure the dish or clothes washer is full before being used.

4 Now have them calculate how much water they saved by limiting their water use. How much water would they be able to save if they did this every day for a year?

Taking Action

1 Have the children come up with a family action plan to encourage water conservation at home. For example they could find out about installing a water-saving showerhead or faucets, or a displacement object in the toilet tank.

2 Help the children find out where their water comes from. If it is piped into the house by the town, have them call the town offices to ask how much the water costs. Usually the cost is by cents per gallon.

3 Have the children calculate how much money the family is spending for water now and how much less it would cost if the family used more conservation techniques.

4 Some ideas that children may suggest are fixing leaky faucets and running toilets, consolidating laundry loads, waiting until the dish washer is full before using it, and other ways of not letting water run unnecessarily.

WATER USE CHARTS

Flushing a standard toilet	6 gallons
Flushing a water-saving toilet	1.5 to 3.5 gallons
Taking a shower.	5 gallons a minute
Taking a bath.	36 gallons
Washing clothes.	35-60 gallons
Washing dishes (*machine*).	10 gallons
Brushing your teeth (*letting water run*)	2 gallons
Washing your hands (*letting water run*)	2 gallons
Watering the lawn.	5-10 gallons a minute

POLLUTION SEARCH
For ages 7 to 11

Materials needed:

Part A: paper, pen or pencil.

Part B: flashlight, white paper strips, petroleum jelly, magnifying glass, baking potatoes, wax paper.

Overview

Here are some ways for children to take a closer look at pollution both indoors and out: what it is, what it looks like, where it comes from, and how to reduce it.

Background

Thick brown haze wrapped around a city. Unwanted tires, appliances, and other refuse floating in a stream. Oil washing up on a beach. All of these are examples of pollution. Human-generated chemicals, trash, noise, and heat can all be pollutants. So can ash spewing from an erupting volcano or smoke spreading from a forest fire. Pollution is any contamination of air, water, or land that affects the outdoor or indoor environment in an unwanted way. Pollution of air, land, and water are found in many ways:

Outdoor Air Pollution: Autos, incinerators, coal-fired power plants and factories, would—if there were no pollution controls—send large amounts of carbon dioxide, sulfur oxides, soot and other pollutants into the air. Fireplaces and wood-burning stoves also add ash and other pollutants to the atmosphere. Other forms of pollution that require strict controls include chlorofluorocarbons (used in refrigerators and air conditioners), and toxins such as benzene and lead.

Indoor Air Pollution: The most common form of indoor air pollution is radon, which occurs naturally in some parts of the country and seeps into houses through the foundation. Other sources of indoor air pollution include paints, pesticides, household cleaners, small leaks from gas appliances as well as some building materials and furnishings which may give off small amounts of harmful vapors. Microscopic organisms like mold, mildew, bacteria, viruses, and dust mites are another form of indoor air pollution. Since houses and apartments are becoming more tightly-sealed to prevent energy waste they are also keeping these pollutants inside our homes.

Water Pollution: In general, pollutants end up in water from being dumped in it, washed into it, or seeped into it through the ground. Fertilizers, pesticides and oil from cars must be used sparingly and carefully (and then disposed of properly) so they do not drain into waterways from farm land, lawns and streets. Sewage treatment plants and industrial plants sometimes discharge pollutants directly into waterways, and oil can seep into water from poorly maintained or damaged ships. Some pollutants fall with rain or snow.

Land Pollution: Everything we throw away has to go somewhere. Much of our solid waste ends up in landfills. Hazardous waste such as chemicals left over from manufacturing processes, flammable liquids, and corrosive material is placed in designated landfills or burned in special incinerators. Radioactive waste and particularly dangerous chemicals are sometimes stored in drums, or injected into deep underground wells.

Pollution Control: By definition pollution is bad. But pollution is unavoidable. Natural events like erupting volcanoes can generate pollution. And, by simply going about our everyday lives, we also pollute. However, we can reduce the amount of pollution by making certain that factories, power plants and solid waste disposal facilities are operated properly— and by modifying our own lifestyles so we consume less power and generate less waste.

Part A: Neighborhood Patrol

Children need to understand that pollution exists in their own environment before they can adopt ways to decrease it. These activities will help children see the pollution around them and begin to show them what they can do to improve their own local environments.

Demonstration 1: *Pollution Detectives*

Pointing out to children what pollution is will let them begin thinking about where it comes from.

1 Talk to the children about what pollution is, using the background provided here. Tell them they are going to try to find pollution and pollutants themselves.

2 Take them on a walk in the neighborhood. Tell them to call out and write down the pollution they see (litter or smoke, for example), hear (honking horns, airplanes) or smell (car fumes, fresh paint, poorly-stored garbage). Have them note where they found the pollution.

3 After you return, have each child read what he or she has written down. Ask the children how they think each pollutant got there. Then ask them if they think there was a way to avoid polluting the neighborhood in each instance. Ask them to think of ways that the pollution could have been avoided. Ask them to think about whether they have ever caused pollution. Could they have avoided doing so?

Part B: Particle Pursuit

Pollution inside the house is also extremely important. Americans spend 80% of their time indoors, eating, sleeping, reading, watching television, working, and so on. These experiments will alert children to pollutants inside their homes and get them thinking about ways to decrease it.

Demonstration 1: *The Air We Breathe*
Pollution creeps into homes through open doors and windows, and tiny cracks in walls. It's hard to realize how much there is until you look for it.

1 Give children a flashlight. Close the blinds, turn on the flashlight, and turn out the lights. Talk about what is seen in the beam of light. Do this in several different parts of the house and talk about what was seen.

2 Make a dozen strips of white paper for each child and have them write their names on each piece. Then tell them to smear a very thin layer of petroleum jelly on one side of each strip. Have them place strips in different locations around the house. Good spots to choose are near windows, in the kitchen, in a closet, in the bathroom.

3 The next day, have each child retrieve their strips. Have them look at what has settled into the petroleum jelly through the magnifying glass. Are there more particles in the strips near windows than the strips that were in the closets? Talk about why this would be so.

Demonstration 2: *Potato Pollution*
Many pollutants are biological pollutants that cause allergies and health hazards. This experiment will determine if any of the particles floating in the air are living organisms.

1 Slice a baking potato into 1/4 inch slices and give each child three or four with an equal number of pieces of wax paper.

2 Wrap one slice up immediately in wax paper and put it into the refrigerator as a control slice.

3 Tell the children to put each slice on a piece of wax paper and put it in a place they already found pollution in previous experiments. The potato will collect particles the same way the petroleum jelly and paper did. The difference is that when the biological pollutants, such as pollen, bacteria, mold, or mildew, land on the potato they will grow into visible colonies of living organisms.

4 Collect the potato slices after a week. Have the children examine them with a magnifying glass, determining if living colonies have begun to grow. Have the children note where these slices were placed, what they see on each, and then have them return the slices from where they had them.

5 Collect the potato slices again after another week. Examine them again. Have the children located potential health hazards by finding the presence of biological pollutants?

Taking Action

1 Allow children to organize a beach, stream or roadside cleanup, with adult help.

2 Let children recycle litter they collect, following local ordinances.

3 Have the children study their indoor pollution notes and determine where the most pollution occurred. Talk about how these pollutant sources could be diminished. Look for ways to improve ventilation without wasting energy through leaky windows.

4 Let children come up with their own ideas of how to decrease air, land, and water pollution and then help them institute the best of these ideas.

ENVIRONMENTAL ACTION PROJECTS

Starting an Environmental Club

Talk to children about the idea of forming an environmental club. You may want to ask another parent to help out, especially if more than ten children are interested.

1 Announce the formation of the club to potentially interested children and parents and arrange an informational meeting.

2 At the first meeting, sign up students and discuss when and where the club will meet. You can brainstorm, as a group, some goals for the club's first activities. Some ideas:

— Energy Awareness Week
— establishment of a community recycling program
— a community clean-up effort

You will have the most success if you start small and "grow" with experience. Encourage club members to plan and execute fun and constructive activities that will generate enthusiasm [and perhaps financial support] — and do something good for the environment.

3 You may want to elect or decide upon club officers. Alternately, children can work as a group, sharing decision-making and responsibilities. The most important thing is to keep everyone involved, focused, and having fun.

Projects for an Environmental Club

Nature Trail

An established nature trail is a good way to prevent people from trampling over tree seedings, ground-nesting animals, and vegetation with low tolerance for foot traffic. Much planning is required before establishing a trail. Topography, soil types, drainage, vegetation and obstacles are some of the considerations to be made, as well as routing the trail to points of interest. Seek professional assistance from your local conservation agencies or scouting groups.

Trails could be surfaced with woodchips or gravel to reduce soil compaction and for ease of walking. You may want to have a nature trail guide, and corresponding numbered markers along the trail.

Bird Station

Install a number of various sized bird houses in this area. Also install a bird feeder, a suet feeder for woodpeckers and a hummingbird feeder. Develop a bird list for this station.

Nesting Boxes

Artificial nesting boxes can be built by students and placed in various locations on your school grounds. This will attract wildlife, and allow students to observe and study nesting characteristics of small animals.

A wildlife biologist can provide specifications and information on what kinds of nesting boxes to build for your area. Wooded fence rows, grassy meadows, forested areas and the banks of ponds and creeks are good locations for nesting boxes.

Animal Tracking Plot

Even an urban area is frequented by many species of wildlife. Birds, mice, squirrels, rabbits, opossums, raccoons and even deer can find themselves at home in the city. Whether you are located in a rural or urban area, an animal tracking plot can yield some interesting tracks to study. An area about three feet or larger is all that is needed to create this feature. The area should be cleared of all grass or other vegetation and filled with sand. Food scraps, grain or other "bait" should then be placed in the middle of the plot regularly to attract wildlife to the area. Children may be surprised at the variety of "critters" right in their own back yard! Plaster casts can be made of tracks.

Wildflower Plot
Wildflowers not only add an attractive atmosphere and aroma to an area, but can be used to produce dyes for fabric or paints. Areas of full sunlight or total shade can both be used to establish plantings of wildflowers. Wildflowers also attract many species of insects and birds for study.

Wildlife Brushpiles
Fallen or pruned limbs and even discarded Christmas trees can be useful building material for wildlife brushpiles. Brushpiles are like natural magnets when it comes to attracting wildlife. Piles should be at least twelve feet (3.6 m) in diameter and five feet (1.5 m) high to be effective.

Plant Succession Areas
By not mowing selected areas of your yard, a greater diversity of plants and plant maturity will occur. This process of gradual (and predictable) replacement of one community of plants and animals by another is referred to as succession. Children can observe and record the various successional stages that will occur.

Guidelines For Requesting Information And Assistance

Be Specific
Your chances of obtaining useful information for your projects will be greatly increased if you state exactly which materials you need, which issues interest you, or what questions you want answered. The "send everything you have" approach is uneconomical and unecological.

Avoid Group-wide Requests
Limit requests for information from any single source to one child and pool the collected data. If you cannot avoid a situation where many children ask for similar information, send all the requests in one envelope and ask that materials returned be mailed in one package to one address.

Request Only What You Need
...and use what you get.

Try Local Sources First
Many community and regional agencies, organizations, and industrial associations can provide valuable information and assistance, particularly on local issues and conditions. Your local librarian can also help locate information available.

Send A Self-Addressed, Stamped Envelope
If you request material or information from volunteer organizations, include a self-addressed stamped envelope. This will bring a quicker response because these organizations have very limited budgets and staff.

Plan On Two To Three Weeks Of Lead Time
If you plan to use the material, such as pamphlet or film, in conjunction with an activity, send your request at least two or three weeks ahead of time.

Make Speaker Requests Well In Advance
Most state agencies and volunteer organizations cannot afford to send their staff or members great distances to speak to one class. However, many resource agencies will assign personnel to meet with children on field trips near their field stations or offices. Most often, the educational experience provided by the presentation in the field is superior to a formal speech.

(Reprinted with permission of American Forest Foundation, Project Learning Tree.)

ADDRESSES FOR ADDITIONAL INFORMATION AND MATERIAL

Air and Waste Management Association , PO Box 2861, Pittsburgh, PA 15230

Alliance for Environmental Education, PO Box 368, The Plains, VA 22171, publishes *Network Exchange*

Aluminum Association, 900 19th Street, Suite 300, Washington, DC 20006

American Forests, PO Box 2000, Washington, DC 20013, publishes *American Forests*

American Forest Foundation, 1111 19th Street, NW, Washington, DC 20036, publishes *Project Learning Tree, Tree Farmer, The Branch*

American Forest and Paper Association, 1111 19th Street, NW, Washington, DC 20036

American Nature Study Society, 5881 Cold Brook Road, Homer NY 13077 publishes *ANSS Newsletter, Nature Study: A Journal of Environmental Education and Interpretation*

The Conservation Foundation, 250 24th Street, NW, Suite 500, Washington DC, 20037, publishes the *CF Letter, Resolve* (Affiliated with World Wildlife Fund - U.S.)

Conservation International, 1015 18th St., NW, Suite 1000, Washington, DC 20036

Council for Solid Waste Solutions, 1275 K Street, NW, Suite 400, Washington, DC 20005

Cultural Survival, 11 Divinity Avenue, Cambridge, MA 02138, publishes *Cultural Survival Quarterly*

Defenders of Wildlife, 1244 19th Street, NW, Washington, DC 20036, publishes *Defenders*

Environmental Action, 6930 Carroll Avenue, Suite 600, Takoma Park, MD 20912, publishes *EnvironmentalAction*

Environmental Defense Fund, 257 Park Avenue South, 16th Floor, New York, NY 10010

Forest History Society, 701 Vickers Avenue, Durham, NC 27701, publishes *Journal of Forest History, Cruiser*

Forestry Canada, Ministry of Natural Resources, Corporate and Public Affairs Directorate, 351 St. Joseph Blvd., Hull, Quebec, KIA 1G5 CANADA

Friends of the Earth, 218 D Street, SE, Washington, DC 20003, publishes *Not Man Apart, Atmosphere*

Girl Scouts of the U.S.A., 420 Fifth Avenue, New York, NY 10018.

Global Network of Environmental Education Centers, 7010 Little River Turnpike, Suite 290, Annandale, VA 22003, publishes *Globe NEEC News*

Izzaak Walton League of America, INC., 1401 Wilson Boulevard, Level B, Arlington, VA 22209, publishes *Outdoor America, Save Our Streams*

Keep America Beautiful, Mill River Plaza, 9 West Broad Street, Stamford, CT 06092

League of Conservation Voters, 1707 L Street, NW, Suite 550, Washington, DC 20036

League of Women Voters of the U.S., 1730 M Street, NW, Washington DC 20036, publishes *The National Voter*

National Arbor Day Foundation, 100 Arbor Avenue, Nebraska City, NE 68410, publishes *Arbor Day*

National Audubon Society, 700 Broadway, New York, NY 10003-9501, publishes *Audubon, Audubon Activist*

National Geographic Society, 17th & M Streets, NW, Washington DC, 20036, publishes *National Geographic* and *World*.

National Park Service, Interior Building., PO Box 37127, Washington, DC 20036.

National Solid Waste Management Association, 1730 Rhode Island Ave., NW, Suite 1000 Washington, D.C. 20036

National Tree Trust, 1001 Pennsylvania Ave., N.W., Suite 1201, Washington DC 20004

The National Wildlife Federation, 1400 16th Street, NW, Washington, DC 20036, publishes *National Wildlife, Ranger Rick, Your Big Yard, NatureScope, International Wildlife, Conservation Directory*

Natural Science for Youth Foundation, 130 Azalea Dr., Roswell, GA, published *Directory of Natural Science Centers*

The Nature Conservancy, 1815 North Lynn Street, Arlington, VA 22209, publishes *The Conservancy News*

North American Association for Environmental Education, 1255 23rd St., NW, Suite 400, Washington, DC 20037, publishes *The Environmental Communicator and offers The Journal of Environmental Education*

Peace Child International, 11426-28 Rockville Pike, Suite 100, Rockville, MD 20852

Population-Environment Balance, 1325 G Street, NW, Suite 1003, Washington, DC 20005, publishes *Balance Report*

Population Reference Bureau, 1875 Connecticut Avenue, NW, Suite 520, Washington DC 20009

Rainforest Alliance, 270 Lafayette Street, Suite 512, New York, NY 10012 publishes *The Canopy*

Resources for the Future, 1616 P Street, NW, Washington, DC 20036

Scientists' Institute for Public Information, 355 Lexington Avenue, 16th Floor, New York, NY 10017, publishes *Environment, SIPISCOPE, Current Controversy*

Sierra Club, 730 Polk Street, San Francisco, CA 94109, publishes *Sierra, National News Report*

Society of American Foresters, 5400 Grosvenor Lane, Bethesda, MD 20814-2197 publishes the *Journal of Forestry*

Soil and Water Conservation Society of America, 7515 NE Ankeny Road, Ankeny, IA 50021, publishes *Journal of Soil and Water Conservation*

U.S. Bureau of Land Management, Department of the Interior, 1849 C. St., NW, Washington, DC 20240

U.S. Department of Agriculture, 14th Street and Indepence Avenue, SW, Washington, DC 20250

USDA Forest Service, Natural Resources and Conservation Education Program, PO Box 96090, Washington DC 20090-6090

USDA Soil Coservation Service, PO Box 2890, Washington, DC 20013-2890

U.S. Environmental Protection Agency, Waterside Mall, 401 M Street, SW, Washington, DC 20250

U.S. Fish and Wildlife Service, Department of the Interior, 1849 C Street, NW, Rm 3445, Washington, DC 20240 or 4401 North Fairfax Drive, Room 452, Arlington, VA 22203

The Wilderness Society, 900 17th Street, NW, Washington, DC 20006, publishes *Wilderness*

Wildlife Conservation International, 185th Street and Southern Boulevard, Bronx, NY 10460 publishes *Wildlife Conservation Magazine, WCI Bulletin*

Wildlife Management Institute, 1101 14th Street, NW, Suite 725, Washington, DC 20005, publishes Outdoor News Bulletin

The Wildlife Society, 5410 Grosvenor Lane, Bethesda, MD 20814-2197, publishes *Journal of Wildlife Management*

World Forestry Center, 4033 SW Canyon Road, Portland, OR 97221

World Resources Institute, 1709 New York Avenue, NW, Washington, DC 20006 publishes *World Resources Report, Environmental Almanac*

Worldwatch Institute, 1776 Massachusetts Avenue, NW, Washington, DC 20036 publishes *Worldwatch Papers, State of the World Series, Worldwatch*

World Wildlife Fund, 1250 24th Street, NW, Suite 500, Washington, DC 20037, publishes *FOCUS, WWF Letter*

Zero Population Growth, 1400 16th Street, NW, Suite 320, Washington, DC 20036, publishes *ZPG Reporter*

FOR MORE INFORMATION

For more information about other educational guides, promotional material and catalogs from Kingfisher, write to:

Larouse Kingfisher Chambers, Inc.
Attn: Marketing Department
95 Madison Avenue
New York, N.Y. 10016
Fax: 212-686-1082
Phone: 800-497-1657

In Canada
Thomas Allen & Son Limited
390 Steelcase Rd.
Markham, Ontario L3R
Fax: 905-475-6747

ACKNOWLEDGMENTS

The activities in this booklet were developed by Project Learning Tree.® Project Learning Tree (PLT), one of the premier environmental educational programs in this country, is co-sponsored by the American Forest Foundation and the Western Regional Environmental Education Council. Project Learning Tree's network of educational workshops has had an enormous impact on environmental education.

Project Learning Tree recently published a 400-page activity guide *Environmental Education Activity Guide (pre-K-8)*, from which the activities in this handbook were excerpted. If you are interested in the PLT or in learning more about their workshop programs, you can contact them at:

Project Learning Tree
1111 19th Avenue N.W.
Washington DC 20036
(202) 463-2462

If you enjoyed doing these exercises, talk to your children about becoming part of the extensive Rescue Mission network sponsored by the United Nations and Peace Child International.

Write to:

Rescue Mission Headquarters, USA
11426-28 Rockville Pike, Suite 100
Rockville, MD 20852

Several times a year interested children will receive the Rescue Mission Action Update, filled with stories about what young people are doing to implement Agenda 21 in different parts of the world. The updates, like Rescue Mission itself, are written, illustrated and edited by children from all over the world. Each update contains a World Wide Action Challenge related to Agenda 21. The first challenge is to make a plan similar to Agenda 21 for a school or neighborhood. Also, included in the newsletters are many ideas and suggestions for pioneering a local Day of Access (see *Rescue Mission*, page 83).

Story contributions from children about local issues will be welcomed for the update newsletter. The newsletter contains details about how children can become involved in writing, editing, and formulating new Action Challenges for the update at the international Rescue Mission headquarters.

Larousse Kingfisher Chambers, Inc.
95 Madison Avenue
New York, NY 10016